Name: _____

Do You Not Agree Waldo

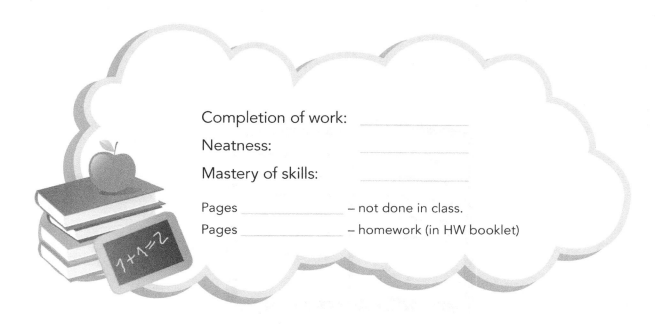

Completion of work: _____

Neatness: _____

Mastery of skills: _____

Pages _____ – not done in class.

Pages _____ – homework (in HW booklet)

Grade: 3
Volume: 1

Parents signature: _____

Reading

Do You Not Agree Waldo

his best tie

gold stripes

"Do you not agree..."

"he makes me feel bad"

green cuffs and gold buttons

toast and jam

the fair

brown velvet

Name: _____   Date: _____

Read the story below and underline all the words that have a long vowel sound in them.

Waldo got dressed to go to the fair. He put on his best tie. On the street he met Homer.

"What a fine tie you have, Waldo," said Homer. "It is red, like mine. But my tie has gold stripes."

"So I see," said Waldo.

"A tie with stripes is better," said Homer. "Do you not agree Waldo?" Homer went on down the street.

"That Homer," said Waldo. "Whatever he has is better."

Waldo got dressed to go to the park. He picked up his best cane. It was made of oak. It had a gold handle. On the street he met Homer.

"What a fine cane you have, Waldo," said Homer. "It is made of oak and has a gold handle, like mine. But my cane has a green stone in the handle."

"So I see," said Waldo.

"A cane with a stone in the handle is better," said Homer. "Do you not agree, Waldo?" Homer went on down the street.

"That Homer," said Waldo. "His tie is better. His cane is better. At times he makes me feel bad."

Waldo got dressed to go to the art show. He put on his best coat. It was made of brown velvet. It had green cuffs and gold buttons. On the street he met Homer.

"What a fine coat you have, Waldo," said Homer. "It is made of brown velvet like mine. It has green cuffs and gold buttons, like mine. But my coat has nine gold buttons. Your coat has just five."

Name: _____　　　**Date:** _____

"So I see," said Waldo.

"A coat with more gold buttons is better," said Homer. "Do you not agree, Waldo?" Homer went on down the street.

"That Homer," Waldo said to himself. "His tie is better. His cane is better. His coat is better. But his manners are not better."

Waldo went for tea. He put on his best vest. He sat at a table outside. He drank tea. He ate toast and jam. He spilled jam on his vest. The jam made red spots. Waldo tried to wipe off the jam. But the spots just got bigger.

Homer came down the street. He saw Waldo. Waldo tried to hide the spots on his vest.

"What a fine vest you have, Waldo," said Homer. "It is pink, like mine. But my vest has no red dots."

"So I see," said Waldo. He waited for Homer to tell him that his vest was better.

"A vest with dots is better," said Homer. "Do you not agree, Waldo?"

"What?" said Waldo. "A vest with spots – I mean dots—is better? You like the dots?"

"Yes," said Homer. "I want a vest with dots. Will you tell me how to get one?"

"Please sit down, Homer," said Waldo. "I will not tell you. I will show you. To show you is better. Do you not agree, Homer?"

Name: _____   Date: _____

Main Events

- Waldo went to the park with his best cane. Homer said that his is better.

- Waldo will show Homer how to get a vest with spots.

- Waldo got dressed to go to the fair with his best tie.

- Waldo got dressed with his best coat to go to the art show, but Homer said his is better.

- Waldo spilled jam on his best vest while he was out for tea.

- Homer told Waldo that his tie with gold stripes is better.

Name: _____　　　**Date:** _____

Sequence of Events Chart

First _____
_____
_____

Then _____
_____
_____

Then _____
_____
_____

Then _____
_____
_____

Then _____
_____
_____

At the end _____
_____
_____

Word Work

B
A
C

Name: _____   Date: _____

Word Work

Connect the syllables to make words found in the story. Then write the words on the lines.

_____

_____

_____

_____

_____

a	vet
him	side
han	ners
vel	gree
out	self
man	dle

Spelling

B
A C

Name: _____   **Date:** _____

Spelling List

<u>Long vowel words</u>

   1. tie

☆ 2. street

☆ 3. like

   4. oak

☆ 5. gold

☆ 6. stone

☆ 7. see

☆ 8. tea

☆ 9. wipe

☆ 10. wait

<u>Extra Credit</u>

   1. rowboat

   2. agree

Use 10 of the spelling words and 1 old spelling word, to fill in the blanks.

- A very valuable form of metal is _____.

- The little boy was wearing a blue suit with a matching blue _____.

- When you need to cross the _____, you must _____ until the red hand turns into a green walking man.

- A diamond is a very valuable _____.

- In the summer my family and I rented a _____ at the lake near my house.

- In the fall you can _____ the leaves on an _____ tree change colors.

- I _____ to drink soda better than iced _____.

- My friend does not _____ with my taste in drinks. He does not like soda at all.

- If you spill your drink be sure to _____ up the mess!

☆ These words will be on the spelling test.

Name: _____   **Date:** _____

Spelling Review Sheet

Word Box

tie   street   like   oak   gold   stone   see   tea   wipe   wait

I. Use the word box to fill in the missing words.

1. My school is located on Oak _____ .

2. The word _____ is also a type of tree.

3. At my school we need to wear a _____ every day.

4. If I forget then I need to _____ at the door for the principal to come and talk to me.

5. Outside there is a garden with a big _____ in the middle.

6. If you stand on top of it you can _____ the whole building.

7. You can see the principal slowly drink his morning _____ as he greets the students.

8. Once it spilled on his _____ watch and I ran to bring him a tissue so he could _____ it off.

9. I really _____ my school, except for this one rule which I think is quite silly.

II. Sort the Spelling Words:

long a	long e	long i	long o

Name: _____   **Date:** _____

Spelling Worksheet

Word Box

tie street like oak gold stone see tea wipe wait agree
rowboat

III. Correct the misspelled words.

schreet _____   stown _____   wayt _____

liyk _____   sea _____   gowld _____

ti _____   tee _____   owk _____

wiyp _____   ugree _____   roebowt _____

IV. Find the synonym (a word that has a similar meaning).

1. rock _____

2. attach _____

3. road _____

4. enjoy _____

5. understand _____

6. clean _____

7. hang on _____

Name: _____   **Date:** _____

Spelling Worksheet

Word Box

tie   street   like   oak   gold   stone   see   tea   wipe   wait

V. Analagies

1. Sidewalk is to walk, as _____ is to ride.

2. Wood is to house, as _____ is to jewelry.

3. Feel is to hands, as _____ is to eyes.

4. Rose is to flower, as _____ is to tree.

5. Play is to park, as _____ is to doctor's office.

VI. Match the words to form compound words.

street   like

wait   pot

gem   light

life   staff

tea   stone

Name: _____   **Date:** _____

A Present for Mom

Completion of work: _____

Neatness: _____

Mastery of skills: _____

Pages _____ – not done in class.

Pages _____ – homework (in HW booklet)

Grade: 3
Volume: 2

Parents signature: _____

Reading

Name: _____   Date: _____

A Present for Mom

she tugged on the sheets

was up in a flash

dashed down the steps

to splash in the warm waves

to hunt for seashells

little ships inside glass bottles

"I can hear the sea,"...

in a second shop

Name: _____   **Date:** _____

Read the story below and underline all the words that have the suffix /ed/. Circle the words that have an /sh/.

"Wake up, Shawn," Mom called as she tugged on the sheets. "It's time for Grandpa to come."

Shawn was up in a flash! He put on shorts and a T-shirt.

Shawn sat on the front steps and waited for Grandpa. At last Shawn saw Grandpa's car drive up. He dashed down the steps and jumped into the car.

"Are you all set to go to the shore?" asked Grandpa.

"Let's go," said Shawn, as he waved to his mom and dad.

Shawn loved the seashore. He liked to splash in the warm waves. He liked to find little fish in the water near the rocks. But most of all, Shawn loved to hunt for seashells.

"Grandpa," Shawn called. "See the shell I picked up!"

Grandpa put the shell up to his ear. "I can hear the sea," he said. Grandpa handed the shell to Shawn.

"Can you hear the sea?" he asked.

Shawn put the shell up to his ear. "Yes, I can hear the sea, too," he said.

"Do you want to visit some of the shops now? Said Grandpa.

"Yes, let's go," said Shawn. "I want to get a present for Mom."

He dropped the shell in the sand and held his grandpa's hand. Grandpa led Shawn to a street of shops. In the first shop they saw little ships inside glass bottles.

Name: _____   **Date:** _____

"No," Shawn said to Grandpa, "ships in bottles are not for Mom."

In a second shop he saw all kinds of T-shirts on a shelf.

"No," said Shawn, "not a T-shirt. Mom has lots of T-shirts."

Shawn and Grandpa went into seven shops. But still, Shawn did not find a present for his mom. The last shop on the street had seashells for sale.

Click! An idea flashed between Grandpa and Shawn. They nodded and winked.

"I hope I can find it, Grandpa," called Shawn.

He ran fast, back to the seashore. Shawn was glad the shell was still in the sand! He picked it up and waved to Grandpa.

"Now she can hear the sea, too," called Shawn. "The seashell is a perfect present for Mom!

Answer the following questions in complete sentences.

1. Where did Shawn go to find a present for Mom? _____

_____

_____

2. Why is the seashell a perfect present? _____

_____

_____

Name: _____　　　　**Date:** _____

Story Mapping

Story Title: _____

Setting – (where and when)

_____

_____

_____

_____

Characters – (who)

_____

_____

_____

_____

Problem – (what problem did the character/s have)

_____

_____

_____

_____

Solution – (how the problem was solved)

_____

_____

_____

_____

Ending – (can be the lesson of the story)

_____

_____

_____

_____

Spelling

ABC

Name: _____   **Date:** _____

Spelling List

Sh words

☆ 1. shirt
2. short
☆ 3. shelf
☆ 4. sheep
5. shore
☆ 6. splash
☆ 7. brush
☆ 8. shell
☆ 9. shake
☆ 10. she

Extra Credit

1. seashell
2. milkshake
3. seashore

Use 9 of the spelling words to fill in the blanks.

One very hot summer day our camp took us on a trip to the _____. Everyone had to take off their shoes and socks and put them on a special _____. There was a lady in charge of all the visiting groups. _____ told us exactly what to do. Next we went down into the water to _____ around and get our feet wet. We were all a bit too _____ to go in too far because then our clothes would get all wet. One boy actually did get his _____ all wet. Then we went out and began to dry up in the sun. When we were pretty dry we went to collect sea _____s. Then we _____ed the sand off of our clothing and went to get our shoes and socks. We were treated to a very cold and refreshing milk _____ which we drank while sitting in a circle and watching the high tide come in. I hope they take us back this summer!

☆ These words will be on the spelling test.

Name: _____   **Date:** _____

Spelling Review Sheet

> Word Box
>
> shirt   short   shelf   sheep   shore   shell   splash   brush   shake   she

I. Fill in the blanks using the words from the word box.

1. The opposite of tall is _____.

2. You can use a special hat _____ to clean your hat.

3. We get wool from a _____.

4. The pronoun used for a girl or lady is _____.

5. You must _____ the bottle of juice before opening it.

6. On Rosh Chodesh the boys all wear a white _____ to school.

7. The books on the top _____ will probably never be read.

8. Babies like to _____ in the water whenever they can.

9. You can see where the sky meets the water if you stand at the

   _____ .

10. When you eat peanuts be sure to remove the _____ .

II. **Sort the Spelling Words:**

R controlled vowels	Short vowels	Long vowels
_____	_____	_____
_____	_____	_____
_____	_____	_____
	_____	

Name: _____   **Date:** _____

Spelling Worksheet

Word Box

shirt short shelf sheep shore shell splash brush shake she

seashell   milkshake   seashore

III. Correct the misspelled words.

schreet _____   stown _____   wayt _____

shert _____   shoort _____   shefl _____

shee _____   sheyp _____   shel _____

shak _____   shoor _____   slpash _____

brosh _____   seeshel _____   miklshk _____

seeshoor _____

IV. Find the synonym (a word that has a similar meaning).

1. beach _____

2. top _____

3. low _____

4. ledge _____

5. wobble _____

6. crust _____

7. spray _____

Name: _____   **Date:** _____

Spelling Worksheet

Word Box

shirt short shelf sheep shore shell splash brush shake she
seashell   milkshake   seashore

V. Complete the analogies using words from the spelling list.

1. Bread is to flour, as milk is to _____.

2. Peel is to orange, as _____ is to peanuts.

3. He is to Chaim, as _____ is to Chaya.

4. Thick is to thin, as tall is to _____.

5. Milk is to cow, as wool is to _____.

VI. Match the words to form compound words. Then write the words on the lines.

milk	brush	1. _____
sea	sleeve	2. _____
sea	shake	3. _____
book	down	4. _____
tooth	shell	5. _____
shirt	shore	6. _____
splash	shelf	7. _____

Word Work

Name: _____   **Date:** _____

Word Work

Connect the syllables to make words found in the story. Then write the words on the lines.

_____

_____

_____

_____

_____

wait	ent
be	ond
hand	fect
per	ed
pres	tween
sec	ed

Split the following compound words into two smaller words;

1. grandpa= _____   _____

2. inside= _____   _____

3. seashells= _____   _____

Name: _____   **Date:** _____

Word Work

Circle the word or words that rhyme with the word in the first box.

share	care	shark	shore
shirt	short	skirt	alert
sheep	shep	creep	heap
shape	shade	tape	abe
wash	slosh	swish	wish
flash	flesh	fish	bash
wish	wash	dish	fish
fresh	flesh	fish	brush

Draw a line to match the picture to the correct word.

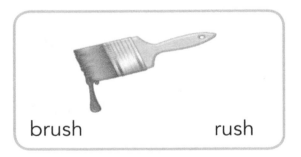

brush   rush

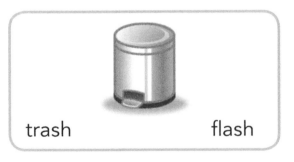

trash   flash

fresh   fish

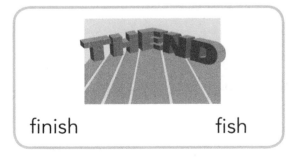

finish   fish

shade   shake

shelf   flesh

Name: _____   **Date:** _____

Out of the Ball Park

Completion of work: _____

Neatness: _____

Mastery of skills: _____

Pages _____ – not done in class.

Pages _____ – homework (in HW booklet)

Grade: 3
Volume: 3

Parents signature: _____

Reading

Out of the Ball Park

to chase balls

forgot to shut the gate

beside three children

the pitcher pitched a ball

in a ditch full of water

watch the rest

to dash after it

the batter

Name: _____   **Date:** _____

Read the story below and underline all the words that have a suffix ed. Circle the words that have the digraph ch, or tch.

Out of the Ball Park

I live with Tess. Tess takes me out with her all the time. She takes me for rides on her bike. She takes me to the park to see the children. She takes me on picnics. But Tess will not take me to ball games.

You see, I like to chase balls. It is so much fun if they go fast.

One day Tess went out to a ball game and forgot to shut the gate. I went to the ball game, too. Tess did not see me go.

At the game, I sat on a bench beside three children. They liked me. They each had a big sandwich and gave me some.

We watched the pitcher pitch a fast ball. I started to dash after it, but the catcher got the ball. After the batter missed three fast balls, he had to sit down.

I saw Tess get up to bat. The pitcher pitched a ball to her, and Tess hit it hard. It shot out of the ball park.

I saw the ball go and chased after it. I watched it land in a ditch full of water. SPLASH! Feet first, into the ditch I jumped. I got the ball and ran back to the park.

I gave the ball to Tess. The children on the benches cheered.

I waited for Tess to tell me I was bad and to send me home, but she didn't.

Name: _____   **Date:** _____

She just gave me a big hug and said, "How did you get to the game, Chuckles? I'm glad you are here. You got the ball for us. Now the game can go on."

Tess let me watch the rest of the game. Now she takes me to all the games.

You see, I don't chase all the balls now. I just chase the balls if they go out of the ball park.

Answer the following questions in complete sentences.

1. How did Chuckles get to the game? _____

_____

_____

2. Why didn't Tess send him home? _____

_____

_____

Main Events

- Chuckles chased after the ball and brought it back to Tess.

- Tess always takes Chuckles to the ball games.

- Tess takes Chuckles out with her all the time but never to a ball game.

- Chuckles went to the ball game when Tess wasn't looking.

- Tess hit a ball out of the ball park and it landed in a ditch of water.

- Tess went to a ball game and forgot to shut the gate behind her.

Name: _____   **Date:** _____

Fill in the sequence of events chart using the main events page. Be sure to put the events in the proper order.

Sequence of Events Chart

First _____
_____
_____

Then _____
_____
_____

Then _____
_____
_____

Then _____
_____
_____

Then _____
_____
_____

At the end _____
_____

Spelling

B
A C

Name: _____   Date: _____

Spelling List

<u>ch, tch words</u>

☆ 1. chin
   2. chase
☆ 3. check
☆ 4. cheek
   5. march
☆ 6. lunch
☆ 7. each
☆ 8. bench
☆ 9. watch
☆ 10. match

<u>Extra Credit</u>

1. chicken
2. chair
3. pitcher

Fill in the blanks using the the spelling words.

The middle meal of the day called _____, is the meal I eat out of my house. At the beginning of every week I _____ the menu with my mother. We look at _____ day to see what will be served. On the days that we will have meat, my mother with not serve _____ for supper. She tries to _____ her supper with my lunch so that we don't have the same thing twice in one day.

In the lunchroom all the boys sit on a _____. The teacher sits on a _____ to _____ us while we eat. Every day a different boy has the job to bring a _____ of water to the table.

One day we had meatballs and spaghetti for lunch. My friend got the sauce all over his _____. When I told him he was dirty he was so embarrassed that his _____ turned red. I felt so bad that I embarrassed him.

After lunch we get to go outside and run around. Some boys like to _____ the birds. I like to play fun ball games with my friends.

☆ These words will be on the spelling test.

Name: _____   Date: _____

Spelling Review Sheet

Word Box

chin cheek check chase bench march lunch watch each match

I. Fill in the blanks using the words from the word box.

1. You can use a _____ to light a fire.

2. Breakfast, _____, and supper are the three main meals.

3. The _____ and the _____ are both parts of our face.

4. You can sit on a _____ when you go to the park.

5. The soldiers learn how to _____ in perfect order when they go to military school.

6. It is amazing to _____ their feet and to see how _____ one moves at exactly the same time.

7. When you go to a store you can pay with cash, a credit card, or a _____.

8. I saw a dog _____ a cat yesterday in the park.

II. Sort the Spelling Words:

ch at the beginning	ch at the end	ch words
_____	_____	_____
_____	_____	_____
_____	_____	_____
_____	_____	

Name: _____

Date: _____

Spelling Worksheet

> Word Box
>
> chin cheek check chase bench march lunch watch each match
> chicken   pitcher   chair

III. Correct the misspelled words.

tchin _____	thase _____	cheak _____
chek _____	mrch _____	luch _____
eatch _____	bentch _____	mach _____
wach _____	chikin _____	picher _____
chare _____		

IV. Find the synonyms (word that has a similar meaning):

1. examine _____

2. every _____

3. seat _____

4. fit _____

5. hunt _____

6. walk _____

7. observe _____

Name: _____   **Date:** _____

Spelling Worksheet

> Word Box
>
> chin cheek check chase bench march lunch watch each match
> chicken   pitcher   chair

V. Find the analogies.

1. Cereal is to breakfast, as sandwich is to _____.

2. Bed is to lay, as _____ is to sit.

3. Thermometer is to temperature, as _____ is to time.

4. Salmon is to fish, as _____ is to bird.

5. Salad is to bowl, as iced tea is to _____.

VI. Match the words to make compound words. Then write the words on the lines.

wrist	mark	1. _____
match	room	2. _____
arm	watch	3. _____
check	chair	4. _____
lunch	box	5. _____
bench	book	6. _____

Word Work

B
A
C

Name: _____   **Date:** _____

Word Work

Syllabication

Connect the syllables to make words found in the story. Then write the words on the lines.

pitch	ed
catch	ture
be	er
start	er
bat	side
pic	ter

_____

_____

_____

_____

_____

Split the following compound words into two smaller words;

1. sandwich= _____   _____

2. beside= _____   _____

3. forgot=_____   _____

Name: _____   Date: _____

Word Work

Circle the word or words that rhyme with the word in the first box.

chair	care	chore	stare
chin	chip	win	spin
chase	race	space	chalk
check	cheek	neck	wreck
cheek	check	week	chick
each	ear	teach	beach
lunch	munch	luck	much
catch	cats	batch	match

Draw a line to match the picture to the correct word.

beach   bench

chore   chair

chicken   kitchen

cheek   check

bunch   bench

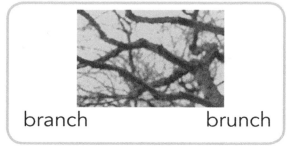

branch   brunch

Name: _____   **Date:** _____

Twin Checkups

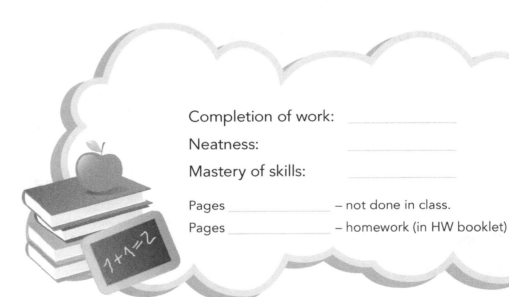

Completion of work: _____

Neatness: _____

Mastery of skills: _____

Pages _____ – not done in class.

Pages _____ – homework (in HW booklet)

Grade: 3
Volume: 4

Parents signature: _____

Reading

Name: _____ **Date:** _____

Twin Checkups

is out of town

another dentist

in the dental chair

peered inside with a little mirror

pictures of your teeth

a little sink beside your chair

Name: _____   **Date:** _____

Read the story below and underline all the words that have a th.

Twin Checkups

"Let's go," Beth said to her brother. "It's time to go to the dentist."

Seth got his coat. "I don't want to go," said Seth. "Dr. North is out of town. I don't want to see another dentist."

Father smiled at the twins. "You will like Dr. Romero," said Father. "You didn't want to meet Dr. North at first. Do you remember?"

"No," Seth said, "I don't remember. I like Dr. North."

"Well, we'll see," said Father. "Let's go. It's time to leave now or we will be late."

The twins were not late. Dr. Romero called Seth first. He sat in the dental chair. The dentist put a dental bib on him.

"How about a ride?" she asked Seth. The chair came up until Seth's face was close to Dr. Romero.

"Open up," said the dentist. "I want to check your teeth." She peered inside with a little mirror. Then she cleaned his teeth.

"Seth, your teeth are fine," said Dr. Romero. "But Dr. North didn't take pictures of your teeth last time. Today I need to take some. The pictures will show your permanent teeth down in your gums. The teeth you have now will come out. Then your big permanent teeth will come in."

Beth had the same checkup as Seth with another dentist. He checked her teeth with a little pick and mirror.

"Now I will clean your teeth," the dentist said.

The dentist cleaned her teeth with an electric dental brush. Then Beth rinsed her teeth with water. She spit into a little sink beside the chair.

Name: _____ **Date:** _____

"Beth, your checkup is finished," the dentist said. "Here is a gift for you. Please clean your teeth with this brush at home."

The children waited on the bench as Father paid the bill.

"Is your dentist's name Dr. Romero?" asked Beth.

"Yes," said Seth, "and I like her. She cleaned my teeth."

That's funny," said Beth. "Dr. Romero is my dentist's name too."

Both dentists came out to speak to father.

"Beth's teeth are fine," said Dr. Romero.

"Seth's teeth are OK, too," said Dr. Romero.

"Are you both Dr. Romero?" asked Seth.

The two dentists winked at the twins. "Yes, and we are twins, too," they said.

Answer the questions in complete sentences.

1. Why didn't Seth want to go to the dentist? _____

_____

_____

2. What happens in a dental checkup? _____

_____

_____

Name: _____　**Date:** _____

Story Mapping

Story Title: _____

Setting – (where and when)

_____

_____

_____

_____

Characters – (who)

_____

_____

_____

_____

Problem – (what problem did the character/s have)

_____

_____

_____

_____

Solution – (how was the problem solved)

_____

_____

_____

_____

Ending – (can be the lesson of the story)

_____

_____

_____

_____

Spelling

Name: _____   **Date:** _____

Spelling List

/th/ words

☆ 1. both

2. think

☆ 3. third

☆ 4. three

5. thick

☆ 6. thank

☆ 7. these

☆ 8. teeth

☆ 9. north

☆ 10. brother

Extra Credit

1. father

2. mother

3. another

Use the spelling list to fill in the missing blanks.

Thanks!

I can _____ of _____

different reasons for which to _____ my

older _____. Firstly, he was the one who

taught me how to punch a ball. Now I can punch it the best in

the whole class. Secondly, he gave me his special compass

which has arrows pointing in every direction (

_____, south, east, and west). The

_____ reason has to do with the way he

always helps me get out of trouble. We were

_____ on our way to school one day when

a dog with big, sharp _____ began to

chase us. He quickly picked up a long, _____

stick and threw it to the dog. The dog began playing

with the stick while we crossed the street without running.

_____ are only some of the reasons why I

owe thanks to my older brother.

_____ important thank you goes out to

my special parents. I would need _____

full page to write only some of the things I am grateful to my

_____ and _____ for. Most

importantly I owe thanks to H-shem for everything I have!

☆ These words will be on the spelling test.

Name: _____   **Date:** _____

Spelling Review Sheet

> Word Box
>
> both think three third thick these teeth north brother thank

I. **Fill in the blanks using the words from the word box.**

1. When you travel from Lakewood to Monsey you need to go
   _____ on the Garden State Parkway.

2. When you travel to Boro Park you need to take _____ bridges.

3. People that travel _____ roads every day, don't even have to
   _____ about where they are going. They know the route in
   their sleep.

4. The _____ day of the week is always Tuesday.

5. When you see very _____ clouds in the sky it is a sign of an
   approaching storm.

6. My older _____ and my older sister will
   _____ become Bar/Bas Mitzvah this year.

7. I need to _____ my dentist for teaching me how to take such
   good care of my _____.

II. **Sort the Spelling Words:**

th at the beginning	th at the end	th in the middle
_____	_____	_____
_____	_____	_____
_____	_____	_____
_____	_____	_____

Name: _____   **Date:** _____

Spelling Worksheet

Word Box
both think three third thick these teeth north brother thank
father   mother   another

III. Correct the misspelled words.

bowth _____   threa _____   teath _____

thik _____   theenk _____   thaynk _____

nurth _____   theyz _____   thurd _____

bruthir _____   fathr _____   unothr _____

muthir _____

IV. Find the Antonyms (a word that means the opposite):):

   1. separately _____

   2. thin _____

   3. south _____

   4. sister _____

   5. ungrateful _____

   6. those _____

   7. the same _____

Name: _____   Date: _____

Spelling Worksheet

Word Box
both think three third thick these teeth north brother thank
father mother another

V. Find the analogies:

1. Smell is to nose, as _____ is to brain.

2. Five is to four, as _____ is to two.

3. Paper is to thin, as cardboard is to _____.

4. Tongue is to taste, as _____ are to chew.

5. East is to west, as _____ is to south.

VI. Connect the syllables to make new words. Then write the words on the lines.
    Some of the words may be compound words.

north	er	1. _____
moth	ly	2. _____
both	east	3. _____
thank	er	4. _____
broth	er	5. _____
third	ful	6. _____

Word Work

Name: _____   **Date:** _____

Word Work

Syllabication

Connect the syllables to make words found in the story. Then write the words on the lines.

_____

_____

_____

_____

_____

check	tle
den	ror
lit	side
mir	up
pic	tist
be	ture

Split the following compound words into two smaller words;

1. checkups= _____   _____

2. beside= _____   _____

3. inside= _____   _____

Name: _____   **Date:** _____

Word Work

Circle the word or words that rhyme with the word in the first box.

thin	chin	thick	think
think	wink	thin	thank
three	the	trees	she
thank	think	tank	bank
this	miss	thin	wish
these	please	this	bees
bath	path	bat	beth
north	fourth	south	worth

Draw a line to match the picture to the correct word.

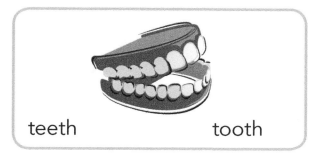

teeth   tooth

west   north

two   three

bath   path

bath   path

think   thank

Name: _____   **Date:** _____

Whales

Completion of work: _____

Neatness: _____

Mastery of skills: _____

Pages _____ – not done in class.

Pages _____ – homework (in HW booklet)

Grade: 3
Volume: 5

Parents signature: _____

Reading

Name: _____   Date: _____

Whales

the biggest animal

a big, dark spot

a hole on top

a stream of fine mist

the biggest and perhaps the smartest

it moves its wide, flat tail

Name: _____   **Date:** _____

A. Reread the story below and underline all the words that have a wh.

Whales

The biggest animal does not live on land. It is a whale, and it lives in the sea.

You can ride on a boat and watch whales. The boat takes you out into the deep parts of the sea.

First you will see a big, dark spot in the water. The whale will swim nearer and nearer to the boat.

Then the whale comes closer to the top of the water. You can see a hole on top of the whale.

SPLASH! SPLASH! The whale comes up to the top of the water. It sends a stream of fine mist up into the air.

The whale takes in air. It moves its wide, flat tail up and sinks into the water.

Down it goes! You have just seen the biggest and perhaps the smartest of all animals.

B. Answer the following questions in complete sentences.

1. Where do whales live? _____

_____

2. How can you watch whales?_____

_____

Name: _____

Date: _____

Interesting Facts

Topic: _____

Fact #1

_____

_____

_____

_____

_____

Fact #2

_____

_____

_____

_____

_____

Fact #3

_____

_____

_____

_____

_____

Fact #4

_____

_____

_____

_____

_____

Most amazing fact:

_____

_____

_____

_____

_____

Spelling

Name: _____   **Date:** _____

Spelling List

<u>wh words</u>

☆ 1. what

☆ 2. when

☆ 3. where

    4. which

☆ 5. white

☆ 6. whale

☆ 7. wheel

☆ 8. while

    9. whine

☆ 10. whisper

<u>Extra Credit</u>

    1. wheelchair

    2. whisker

Use 9 of the spelling words to fill in the missing blanks.

There are many amazing facts to be learned about the fascinating animal the _____. There are many different types of whales to study. You can learn _____ type is nicknamed the killer whale, and _____ the different types of whales live. You can learn _____ these incredible animals eat.

Whales have a blowhole on the top of their heads which helps them breathe _____ under water. You can see an upward spray of water coming from that hole. From far it looks almost like a _____ mist shooting up from the water.

_____ they want to talk to another whale they have their own language in a song-like manner. Some whales have a very loud voice which can be heard for many miles. Other whales make small click-like sounds. Similarly humans tell a lot by the tone of voice in which they speak such as a _____ or a _____.

These are just some interesting facts about whales. Read up about whales and share with your class something new that you learn.

☆ These words will be on the spelling test.

Name: _____   **Date:** _____

Spelling Review Sheet

> Word Box
>
> **what   when   where   which   white   whale   wheel   while   whine   whisper**

I. Fill in the blanks using the words from the word box.

1. To speak in a quiet voice is to speak in a _____. To _____ is to complain in an unreasonable, or irritating way.

2. The color which has all the other colors in it is the color _____.

3. The question word _____ will get an answer that tells the time, the day, or the year.

4. The question word _____ will get an answer that tells a place.

5. _____ high-way do you take when you travel to Boro Park?

6. _____ is the name of your new baby?

7. You can go _____ watching on a special boat that goes out to the ocean. You may have to wait quite a _____ before you actually get to see one.

8. The steering _____ of the car is used to turn the tires in the right direction.

II. Sort the Spelling Words:

Question words;	Words that tell what;	Words that tell how;
_____	_____	_____
_____	_____	_____
_____	_____	_____

Name: _____   **Date:** _____

Spelling Worksheet

Word Box

what when where which white whale wheel while whine whisper
wheelchair   whisker

III. Correct the misspelled words.

wut _____   wen _____   weer _____

wich _____   wiyt _____   wyael _____

weel _____   wiyel _____   wine _____

wisper _____   wealchear_____   wisker_____

IV. Some of the words in the spelling list are homonyms (words which have the
same spelling or sound as another word). Read the phrases below and write
the homonym that it describes.

1. to put clothing on   _____

2. a question asking about a place   _____

3. a question asking to choose one from others   _____

4. somebody who is supposed to have magical powers   _____

5. a drink made from grapes   _____

6. to complain in an unreasonable and irritating way   _____

Homonyms

whine   which   where   witch   wear   wine

Name: _____   **Date:** _____

Spelling Worksheet

> Word Box
>
> what when where which white whale wheel while whine whisper
> wheelchair   whisker

V. Find the analogies:

1. Who is to a person, as _____ is to a time.

2. Dark is to light, as black is to _____.

3. Orange is to tiger, as grey is to _____.

4. Shout is to loud, as _____ is to low.

5. Elephant is to tusk, as cat is to _____.

VI. Connect the syllables to make compound words. Then write the words on the lines.

some	where	1. _____
some	chair	2. _____
wheel	fish	3. _____
what	wheel	4. _____
cart	ever	5. _____
white	what	6. _____

Word Work

Name: _____   **Date:** _____

Word Work

Syllabication

Connect the syllables to make words found in the story. Then write the words on the lines.

_____

_____

_____

_____

_____

big	per
near	haps
clos	to
whis	est
in	er
per	gest

Split the following compound words into two smaller words;

1. wheelchair= _____   _____

2. into= _____   _____

3. rowboat= _____   _____

Name: _____

Date: _____

Word Work

Circle the word or words that rhyme with the word in the first box.

what	when	shut	rat
when	then	where	what
where	there	share	when
which	switch	what	pitch
white	polite	fight	while
while	white	smile	dial
whale	wheel	scale	what
wheel	well	steel	feel

Draw a line to match the picture to the correct word.

wheel   well

wheel   whale

wheelchair   bike

black   white

whisper   whisker

whisper   whisker

Name: _____   **Date:** _____

Riddle-Diddle-Diddle

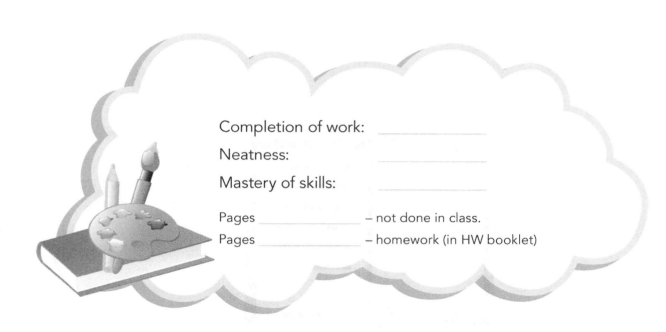

Completion of work: _____

Neatness: _____

Mastery of skills: _____

Pages _____ – not done in class.

Pages _____ – homework (in HW booklet)

Grade: 3
Volume: 6

Parents signature: _____

Reading

Name: _____   **Date:** _____

Riddle-Diddle-Diddle

What did the quilt tell the bed?

_____

Why are the letters q and u like a sock and a shoe?

_____

What do ducks eat with cheese?

_____

When is a quart of milk the freshest?

_____

Spelling

Name: _____ **Date:** _____

Spelling List

qu words

☆ 1. quick

☆ 2. quit

☆ 3. quilt

☆ 4. quack

☆ 5. quite

☆ 6. queen

☆ 7. squint

8. squeal

9. square

10. squash

Extra Credit

1. quiet

2. question

3. squirrel

Fill in the blanks using the words from the spelling list.

A squirrel is a very _____ moving animal. Sometimes while it crosses the street it seems to _____ crossing and turns back. It may do so to confuse the oncoming car. Unfortunately though, the car can _____ it with its tires if it can't stop fast enough. This happens _____ often around here because we have so many squirrels. You might hear a _____ of the tires as a driver tries to stop at the last minute. When it is sunny outside the driver of a car may need to _____ in order to see where he is going. He might miss the crossing _____ in such an event.

The size of a squirrel's brain is about the size of a _____ bee. They are probably not the smartest animals around. A squirrel needs about one pound of food a week to maintain an active life. They don't make much noise as they scurry about in search of food. They are actually pretty _____. If you have any _____ about the life of the squirrel try to find a book that tells about squirrels and read about them.

☆ These words will be on the spelling test.

Name: _____   Date: _____

Spelling Review Sheet

Word Box

quick quit quilt quack quite queen squint squeal square squash

I. Fill in the blanks using the words from the word box.

1. Every set of linen comes with a pillowcase, sheet, and _____ cover.

2. The king and his _____ live in a grand palace.

3. The duck in my pond likes to _____ loudly all day.

4. The baby will _____ with delight when I show her the new toy.

5. My bedroom has four walls that are the same size. Its in the shape of a _____.

6. The _____ and the cucumber are two vegetables that are commonly confused.

7. One who is _____ to _____ will never find success.

8. It can be _____ difficult to try again after you fail.

9. If you wear sunglasses on a sunny day you will be able to see without having to _____ your eyes.

II. Sort the Spelling Words:

qu words;	squ words
_____	_____
_____	_____
_____	_____
_____	_____
_____	_____

Spelling Worksheet

Word Box

quick quit quilt quack quite queen squint squeal square squash
quiet question squirrel

III. Correct the misspelled words.

kwack _____   kwilt _____   kwite _____

kwit _____   kwick _____   kween _____

skwint _____   skwirel _____   skwash _____

skwear _____   kwiet _____   kweshton _____

IV. Find the synonym (word with a similar meaning)

1. a peek _____

2. very _____

3. rapid _____

4. leave _____

5. cover _____

6. squeeze _____

7. silence _____

Spelling Worksheet

Word Box

quick quit quilt quack quite queen squint squeal square squash
quiet question squirrel

V. **Find the analogies:**

1. Turtle is to slow, as rabbit is to _____.

2. Circle is to oval, as _____ is to rectangle.

3. Meow is to cat, as _____ is to duck.

4. Problem is to solution, as _____ is to answer.

5. A man is to his hat, as a _____ is to her crown.

VI. **Connect the syllables to make compound words. Then write the words on the lines.**

quick	able	1. _____
earth	ball	2. _____
question	sand	3. _____
head	quake	4. _____
racquet	quarters	5. _____

Word Work

B
A
C

Name: _____   Date: _____

Word Work

Syllabication

Connect the syllables to make words found in the story. Then write the words on the lines.

_____

_____

_____

_____

_____

_____

qui	ter
ques	ly
quack	et
quart	ers
squir	tion
quick	rel

Split the following compound words into two smaller words;

1. earthquake= _____   _____

2. headquarters= _____   _____

3. cheesecake= _____   _____

Name: _____   **Date:** _____

Word Work

Circle the word or words that rhyme with the word in the first box.

squeak	tweak	cheek	quack
quack	track	quick	walk
quick	thick	wick	chick
squeal	wheel	peel	heal
quit	flight	quite	fit
quite	fight	quit	split
queer	there	chair	share
squirt	shirt	skirt	short

Draw a line to match the picture to the correct word.

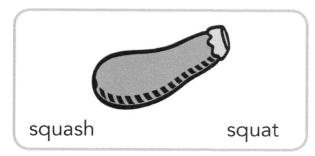

squash   squat

quilt   quit

queer   queen

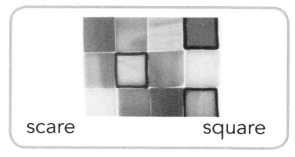

scare   square

squirt   squint

quite   quiet

Name: _____   **Date:** _____

The Little Red Hen and the Fox

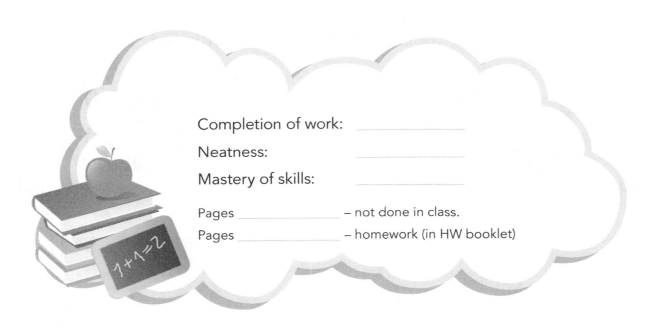

Completion of work: _____

Neatness: _____

Mastery of skills: _____

Pages _____ – not done in class.

Pages _____ – homework (in HW booklet)

Grade: 3
Volume: 7

Parents signature: _____

Reading

Name: _____   **Date:** _____

The Little Red Hen and the Fox

behind a tall box next to the stove

a wonderful dinner

she had left a window open

if I am quiet

into her apron pocket

will taste wonderful

with her hands on her hips

six more quarts of water

Thump! Splash!

a little bigger than herself

a big load

fell fast asleep

Name: _____   **Date:** _____

Reread the story below and underline all the words that are spelled with the letter x.

The Little Red Hen and the Fox

Narrator One: One day a fox wanted his dinner. He said to Mother Fox:

Fox: What do we have for dinner?

Mother Fox: We ate all there was at lunchtime. There is not a bite or a sip left.

Fox: Then mix salt and pepper in a pot of water. Put it on the stove to get hot. I will go after the little red hen.

Narrator Two: So off went the fox. On his back he had a sack to put the hen in.

Narrator Three: Little Red Hen had gone out to find bugs to eat. The fox saw that she had left a window open. He slipped inside and hid behind a tall box next to the stove.

Fox: When Little Red Hen comes back, I must be quick to catch her. She will make a wonderful dinner!

Narrator One: Little Red Hen came home. She stepped inside.

Little Red Hen: Home again, Home again! Now I will fix these six fat bugs for dinner.

Narrator Two: As quick as a flash, the fox jumped out and grabbed Little Red Hen.

Fox: Ah, ha! I have you, Little Red Hen! Now I will stuff you into this sack. Later you will be a wonderful dinner!

Narrator Three: The fox started for home. Little Red Hen was a big load. The fox had to stop beside the road to rest. He was so tired that he fell fast asleep.

Little Red Hen: What luck! The fox is fast asleep. If I am quiet, I can escape from this sack.

Narrator One: She reached into her apron pocket.

Name: _____   Date: _____

Little Red Hen: I will cut a hole in the sack!

Narrator Two: Snip, snip, snip. Little Red Hen was free at last.

Little Red Hen: Now I need to find a stone as big as I am. Then I will put the stone inside the sack and close the hole.

Narrator Three: She saw a stone just a little bigger that herself. Little Red Hen then rolled the stone into the sack. Then she reached into her apron pocket for her needle. She closed up the sack and ran for home.

Narrator One: After a while, the fox woke up.

Fox: Oh no! I didn't mean to fall asleep! I must get home fast.

Narrator Two: The fox began to drag the sack.

Fox: This sack is so hard to pull. What a fat hen she must be. She will taste wonderful!

Narrator Three: At last the fox reached home with his sack. Mother Fox waited by the fire with her hands on her hips.

Mother Fox: Where have you been? You are so late, I had to get six more quarts of water to fill the pot!

Narrator One: The fox saw that the water in the pot was hot.

Fox: Quick! Let's put the little red hen in the pot. You hold the cover while I dump her in.

Narrator Two: THUMP! SPLASH! The fox and his mother jumped back from the pot.

Mother Fox: That's not a fat hen! That's a big stone!

Fox: Little Red Hen has tricked us! And now we have no dinner to eat!

Narrator Three: Meanwhile, Little Red Hen sat in her snug little home. She had six fat bugs for dinner. And the fox never bothered her again.

How many did you find? _____

Name: _____   **Date:** _____

Answer the following questions in complete sentences.

1. Why did the fox want to catch the little red hen? _____

_____

2. How did she trick the fox? _____

_____

Name: _____   **Date:** _____

Story Mapping

Main Character;

_____

Supporting Characters;

_____
_____
_____
_____

Setting

When _____
_____
_____
_____
_____

Where _____
_____
_____
_____

Story Title

_____

Solution

_____
_____
_____
_____
_____
_____
_____
_____
_____

Problem _____
_____
_____
_____
_____
_____
_____
_____
_____

Spelling

ABC

Name: _____   Date: _____

Spelling List

Words with x

1. six
2. fix
3. mix
4. fox
5. foxes
6. boxes
7. ax
8. relax
9. taxi
10. exit

Extra Credit

1. exam
2. extra

Spot 10 misspelled spelling words in the passage below. Draw a line through the word and write the correct spelling on top.

It has long been believed that the ~~foks~~ fox is a sly animal. If you read books about foxes you will learn the truth. If you see a fox you can reelax because foxez generally don't hurt people. There have actually been far more attacks from dogs than from foxes. Many children stories talk about the fox that is trying to outsmart other smaller animals. This may be true because foxes do eat other animals. When they are not hungry they may still kill other animals for ekschra food and save it for later. They will bury it in the ground or under snow. Some foxes actually eat a lot of foods including different types of animals and fruits and vegetables.

When a fox is used as a character in a story he is like a person. There is a story in which a woodchopper came with his aksx to kill the bad fox who dressed up like an old grandmother. The fox only wanted to eat the boxiz of cookies that the little girl brought for her sick grandmother. In the story the fox was mean and would not let the little girl eggzit the house. Now that we know the truth about foxes we can make up a new ending to the story. The fox apologized and even called a taxy for the girl to take her home. He wanted to fiks his problem so he gave her siks dollars to buy new cookies.

It is fun to make up stories! Try making up one of your own about the good old fox.

Name: _____   **Date:** _____

Spelling Review Sheet

> Word Box
>
> fix   mix   fox   foxes   boxes   ax   relax   taxi   six   exit

I. Fill in the blanks using the words from the word box.

1. A great way to _____ is to go boating on a nice calm lake.

2. The world was created in _____ days.

3. In every building you will see the word _____ in big red letters on top of every doorway.

4. It is fun to watch how the flour, sugar, eggs, cocoa, and other ingredients _____ together to become a cake.

5. You would go to a car mechanic to _____ your car.

6. One _____ was looking for food to bring back to the other _____ in his family.

7. The wood chopper used a strong _____ to chop the trees into firewood.

8. A _____ driver needs to have a very good sense of direction.

9. The family packed all their belongings into one hundred brown _____.

II. Sort the Spelling Words:

One syllable words	Two syllable words
_____	_____
_____	_____
_____	_____
_____	_____

Name: _____   **Date:** _____

Spelling Workheet

Word Box

fix   mix   fox   foxes   boxes   ax   relax   taxi   six   exit

exam   extra

III. Correct the misspelled words.

fiks _____   miks _____   bokses _____

foksiz _____   foks _____   aks _____

relaks _____   taksi _____   eggzit _____

siks _____   ekstra _____   egzam _____

IV. Find the synonym (word with a similar meaning)

1. repair   _____

2. combine   _____

3. cartons   _____

4. unwind   _____

5. cab   _____

6. leave   _____

7. test   _____

8. spare   _____

Name: _____   **Date:** _____

Spelling Workheet

Word Box

fix   mix   fox   foxes   boxes   ax   relax   taxi   six   exit
exam   extra

V. **Find the analogies:**

1. Two is to three, as _____ is to seven.

2. Police car is to blue, as _____ is to yellow.

3. Cat is to tiger, as dog is to _____.

4. Find is to lost, as _____ is to broken.

5. Wednesday is to work, as Shabbos is to _____.

VI. **Connect the words to make compound words. Then write the words on the lines.**

sand	payer	1. _____
text	teen	2. _____
tax	box	3. _____
fox	book	4. _____
six	hole	5. _____

Word Work

Name: _____　　**Date:** _____

Word Work

Syllabication

Connect the syllables to make words found in the story. Then write the words on the lines.

nar	der	cape
din	ra	ful
win		ner
won		dow
a		tor
es		sleep

_____

_____

_____

_____

_____

Split the following words into two smaller parts;

1. started= _____　_____

2. pocket= _____　_____

3. herself= _____　_____

Name: _____   **Date:** _____

Word Work

Circle the word or words that rhyme with the word in the first box.

fax	wax	flax	fox
fix	fox	picks	six
box	socks	mix	fox
flex	flags	checks	exit
tux	tax	trucks	luck
pinch	pitch	bench	flinch
bench	wrench	pinch	quench
pitch	rich	which	kitchen
path	math	with	both

Draw a line to match the picture to the correct word.

fox   fix

socks   six

back   box

ox   axe

ax   ox

relax   exit

Name: _____   **Date:** _____

The Beekeeper

Completion of work: _____

Neatness: _____

Mastery of skills: _____

Pages _____ – not done in class.

Pages _____ – homework (in HW booklet)

Grade: 3
Volume: 8

Parents signature: _____

Reading

Name: _____   Date: _____

The Beekeeper

the slide show on bees

will zigzag and buzz from blossom to blossom

pollen sticks to her fuzz

into little pockets on her hind legs

the bee takes the pollen back to the hive

she does not have time to feed or clean herself

one queen and lots of bees that help her

"bees make a thick, sweet liquid and store it in the hive"

Name: _____   Date: _____

Reread the story below, The Beekeeper. Underline any phrase you recognize from preparation for reading. Circle all the words that have the /z/ sound in it. You can circle words that have an s which sounds like a z.

Val's brother James stopped to see the wild animals. But Val wanted to see the slide show on bees. She yelled to her brother. "Let's go inside now!"

"You are just in time," said Miss Fox. "Find two seats and relax, and we can begin."

"I'm Helen Fox, and I am a beekeeper," she explained. "Feel free to speak to me while I show the slides."

"This is a female bee," began Miss Fox. "It is the kind you see in most gardens. She will zigzag and buzz from blossom to blossom. She takes a sweet drink from each one."

"As she works, pollen sticks to her fuzz. She brushes the pollen into little pockets on her hind legs. The bee takes the pollen back to the hive, and she feeds it to the little bees."

"The biggest bee in the slide is the queen," explained Miss Fox. "She's the mother of all the bees in the hive. Her job is to make eggs. She does not have time to feed or clean herself. The other bees must take care of her."

"These boxes are beehives," Miss Fox went on. "In each hive lives one queen and lots of bees that help her.

"Inside the hive are frames which the bees fill with wax. This slide shows a frame from inside a hive.

"The bees form the wax into six-sided shapes," explained Miss Fox. "Then the queen bee drops an egg into each one."

"Bees make a thick, sweet liquid and store it in the hive," Miss Fox told them. "This is a jar of it. Do you want to taste some?"

How many words with a /z/ sound did you find? _____

Name: _____   **Date:** _____

Answer the following questions in complete sentences.

1. Who is the biggest bee? _____

_____

2. How do the bees take care of her? _____

_____

Name: _____   **Date:** _____

Topic _____

K - What do I already know about this topic?	**W** - What do I want to find out?	**L** - What have I learned about this topic?
_____	_____	_____
_____	_____	_____
_____	_____	_____
_____	_____	_____
_____	_____	_____
_____	_____	_____
_____	_____	_____
_____	_____	_____
_____	_____	_____

Spelling

B
A C

Name: _____   **Date:** _____

Spelling List

<u>Words with z</u>

☆ 1. zipper

☆ 2. zero

☆ 3. zebra

☆ 4. fuzz

☆ 5. buzz

☆ 6. froze

☆ 7. sneeze

8. squeeze

9. breeze

10. freeze

<u>Extra Credit</u>

1. please

2. does

☆ 3. was

Use the spelling words to fill in the blanks.

- A _____ is a black and white striped animal.

- A _____ is used to close things.

- The score was _____ to one.

- Water will _____ into ice if it is placed in the freezer.

- Bees will _____ when they are excited.

- "_____ tells us a scary story", the children begged.

- You can feel a soft _____ if you touch a peach with your fingers.

- You can feel a _____ if you are outside on a windy day.

- Black pepper makes me _____.

- If you _____ a lemon you will get some lemon juice.

- The water in the lake _____ last night when the temperature hit a very low number.

- Where _____ the president of the United States live?

- George Bush _____ the president before Barack Obama.

☆ These words will be on the spelling test.

Name: _____   **Date:** _____

Spelling Review Sheet

> Word Box
> zipper zero zebra sneeze froze freeze squeeze buzz fuzz breeze

I. **Fill in the blanks using the words from the word box.**

1. If you go to visit the safari you may see a _____.

2. When my family travels together in one car we all have to _____ together to make room for everybody.

3. The lake will _____ this winter, just like it _____ last winter.

4. Another word for nothing is _____.

5. Some door bells sound like a _____.

6. The words does, buzz and _____ all rhyme.

7. Be sure to _____ your coat so you don't feel the cold _____.

8. To prevent the spread of germs, cover your nose and mouth whenever you

   _____.

II. **Sort the Spelling Words:**

One syllable words	Two syllable words
_____	_____
_____	_____
_____	_____
_____	
_____	
_____	

III. **Write the words that end with a z sound (not extra credit words):**

_____, _____, _____, _____,

_____, _____, _____, _____.

Circle the letter that comes after the z (it can be another z).

Name: _____   Date: _____

Spelling Workheet

> Word Box
>
> zipper zero zebra sneeze froze freeze squeeze buzz fuzz breeze
> please   does   was

III. Correct the misspelled words.

zippor _____   zerow _____   zeebru _____

sneez _____   frowz _____   freez _____

skweez _____   buz _____   fuz _____

breez _____   duz _____   pleez _____

wuz _____

IV. Find the synonym (word with a similar meaning)

1. nothing _____

2. ring _____

3. gentle wind _____

4. ice up _____

5. make happy _____

6. squash _____

7. closure _____

Name: _____   **Date:** _____

Spelling Workheet

> Word Box
>
> zipper zero zebra sneeze froze freeze squeeze buzz fuzz breeze
> please   does   was

V. Find the analogies:

1. Nothing is to _____, as 100 is to excellent.

2. Lion is to _____ , as cow is to chicken.

3. Tissue is to _____ , as napkin is to spill.

4. Melted is to _____ , as oil is to gas.

5. Fingers are to _____ , as feet are to walk.

6. Soft is to _____ , as rough is to brick.

7. Bees are to _____ , as cats are to meow.

8. Wind is to _____ , as clouds are to rain.

VI. Connect the syllables to make words. Then write the words on the lines.

ze	zer	1. _____
zip	zen	2. _____
buz	bra	3. _____
fro	zag	4. _____
zig	per	5. _____

Word Work

ABC

Name: _____   **Date:** _____

Phonics Sheet

Syllabication: Chunk each word into smaller parts. (Hint; spot the vowels first). Each part should have a vowel and a consonant after it.

words	syllable 1	syllable 2	syllable 3
backpack	back	pack	
animals	an	i	mals
zizag	zig	zag	
blossom			
pollen			
pockets			
liquid			
upset			
picnic			

Which type of vowel does each part in the words above have? short or long

Word Work

Suffixes and Root Words: Chunk each word into suffixes and root words.

words	root word	suffix
stopped	stop	ed
wanted		
yelled		
explained		
slides		
works		
brushes		
biggest		
boxes		
frames		

Which words have a double consonant before the suffix?_____

Do you know the rule?

Name: _____   Date: _____

Word Work

Circle the word or words that rhyme with the word in the first box.

buzz	fuzz	does	fiz
please	breeze	squeeze	buzz
froze	those	hose	loss
zipper	pepper	slipper	size
sneeze	snap	cheese	knees
zip	slip	zap	chop
zero	zip	hero	share
wild	while	child	mild
slides	slide	rides	pride

Draw a line to match the picture to the correct word.

zero   hero

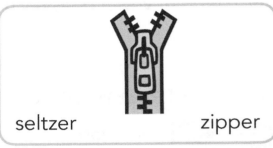

seltzer   zipper

zigzag   ziploc

Horse   zebra

frozen   freezer

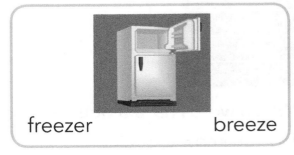

freezer   breeze

Name: _____   **Date:** _____

Best Pals

Completion of work: _____

Neatness: _____

Mastery of skills: _____

Pages _____ – not done in class.

Pages _____ – homework (in HW booklet)

Grade: 3
Volume: 9

Parents signature: _____

Name: _____   **Date:** _____

Best Pals

wandering off too far

in one leap

thick branches of the pine trees

like long hands and fingers

reaching out to grab him

broken boards, cans, bottles, boxes...

Mike and Fletcher disagreed

Name: _____   **Date:** _____

Reread the story below, Best Pals. Underline any phrase you recognize from preparation for reading. Circle all the words that have /ng/ in it.

Fletcher came out onto the front porch, banging the screen behind him. "Fletch," his father called to him from the kitchen. "Don't go wandering off too far. I want you back home before dark."

"I'm just going over to Mike's," Fletcher called back, jumping down the steps in one leap. "We're fixing up an old shed for Mike's horse."

Mike Wilson lived down the road a mile, just on the other side of the pine forest. Fletcher liked Mike a lot, but he hated that pine forest.

Fletcher walked along the side of the road until he came to the forest. Then he stopped and stared. Even in the daytime, the thick branches of the pine trees were dark. Deep in the forest it was darker still.

Fletcher shivered. Stuffing his hands in his pockets, he started walking fast.

The dark branches were swinging in the breeze. They seemed like long hands and fingers reaching out to grab him. Fletcher walked in the middle. Keeping his eyes on the road in front of him, he walked faster and faster.

At last, Fletcher saw Mike standing on his front porch. Mike Wilson was Fletcher's best pal. But Fletcher had never told his pal how scared he was of the pine forest.

"Let's go," said Mike. "We have lots to do before it gets dark."

The shed was full of things to clean out—old papers, broken boards, cans, bottles, boxes, and an old trunk.

Sometimes Mike and Fletcher disagreed. When Fletcher tried to move the trunk, Mike got mad and started yelling, "What are you doing? I don't want it there!"

Fletcher got mad and started yelling, too.

"You're impossible!" he screamed at Mike and stomped out of the shed.

Name: _____   **Date:** _____

Fetcher ran down the path and onto the road. It was almost dark now. He started walking fast, kicking at stones and muttering to himself. He was so mad at Mike that he never even saw the dark pine forest on both sides of the road.

In no time he was home. He stared back at the dark forest. Then he clapped his hands and ran into the kitchen.

"Dad, can I call up Mike?" he asked.

"But you just saw him," his father said.

"But Dad," Fletcher said, "Mike's my best pal. I've got something important to tell him."

How many words with a /z/ sound did you find? _____

Answer the following questions in complete sentences.

1. Why did Fletcher hate the pine forest? _____

_____

2. What do you think Fletcher told Mike? _____

_____

Name: _____   **Date:** _____

Story Mapping

Main Character;

_____

Supporting Characters;

_____

_____

_____

_____

Setting

When _____

_____

_____

_____

_____

Where _____

_____

_____

_____

Story Title

_____

Solution

_____

_____

_____

_____

_____

_____

_____

_____

Problem _____

_____

_____

_____

_____

_____

_____

_____

Spelling

Name: _____   **Date:** _____

Spelling List

<u>Digraph review</u>

1. square
2. squash
⭐ 3. these
⭐ 4. thank
⭐ 5. north
⭐ 6. watch
⭐ 7. ditch
⭐ 8. branch
⭐ 9. short
⭐ 10. splash

<u>Extra Credit</u>

1. September
2. cheese
3. father

Use the spelling words to fill in the blanks.

- A large green vegetable which can be confused with a cucumber is a _____.

- The opposite of tall is _____.

- A shape with four equal sides is a _____.

- When somebody gives you a gift it is proper to _____ them.

- One of the four directions is _____.

- A car can get stuck in a _____ which is a hole in the street.

- Monkeys in the zoo jump from _____ to branch.

- Babies like to _____ and play in the bathtub while bathing.

- A _____ is a clock you can wear on your hand.

- _____ sentences all have one word from this week's spelling list.

⭐ These words will be on the spelling test.

Name: _____   **Date:** _____

Spelling Review Sheet

Word Box
square squash these thank north watch ditch branch short splash

I. **Fill in the blanks using the words from the word box.**

1. This word rhymes with wash. _____ This word begins like wash. _____

2. This word rhymes with crash. _____

3. This word rhymes with forth. _____

4. This word rhymes with bank. _____

5. This word rhymes with please. _____

6. This word rhymes with share. _____ This word begins like share. _____

7. This word rhymes with pitch. _____

8. Bran + ch = _____ .

II. **Sort the Spelling Words:**

Words with qu	Words with th	Words with sh	Words with ch, tch
_____	_____	_____	_____
_____	_____	_____	_____
_____	_____	_____	_____

Name: _____   **Date:** _____

Spelling Workheet

Word Box

square squash these thank north watch ditch branch short splash
September cheese father

III. Correct the misspelled words.

skwear _____   skwash _____   theez _____

thaynk _____   noorth _____   wach _____

dich _____   branch _____   shoort _____

splash _____   spetmbr _____   cheez _____

fathr _____

IV. Find the synonym (word with a similar meaning)

1. squeeze   _____

2. observe   _____

3. dump   _____

4. twig   _____

5. small   _____

6. spray   _____

7. appreciate   _____

Spelling Workheet

> Word Box
>
> square squash these thank north watch ditch branch short splash
> September cheese father

V. Find the analogies:

1. South is to _____ , as east is to west.

2. Time is to _____ , as temperature is to thermometer.

3. Apple is to fruit, as _____ is to vegetable.

4. Circle is to oval, as _____ is to rectangle.

5. Tall is to _____ , as thick is to thin.

6. Sift is to sand, as _____ is to water.

7. Hand is to person, as _____ is to tree.

VI. Connect the syllables to make words. Then write the words on the lines.

th	a sh	1. _____
s qu	th	2. _____
s qu	ank	3. _____
n or	n ch	4. _____
b r a	are	5. _____

Word Work

Name: _____   **Date:** _____

Word Work

Syllabication: Chunk each word into smaller parts. (Hint; spot the vowels first). Each part should have a vowel and a consonant after it.

words	syllable 1	syllable 2	syllable 3
Wilson	Wil	son	
kitchen			
upset			
welcome			
catnip			
satin			
seven			
insist			
wagon			

Which type of vowel does each part in the words above have?

short or long

Name: _____   **Date:** _____

Word Work

Suffixes and Root Words: Chunk each word into suffixes and root words.

words	root word	suffix
banging	bang	ing
wandering		
jumping		
fixing		
stuffing		
walking		
swinging		
reaching		
keeping		
standing		

Which type of vowel does each part in the words above have?

short or long

Name: _____   **Date:** _____

The Singing King

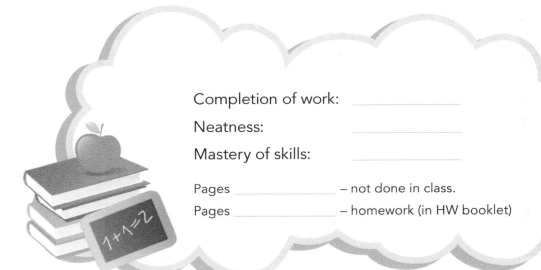

Completion of work: _____

Neatness: _____

Mastery of skills: _____

Pages _____ – not done in class.

Pages _____ – homework (in HW booklet)

Grade: 3
Volume: 10

Parents signature: _____

Reading

Name: _____ **Date:** _____

The Singing King

his singing was awful

squawks like a chicken

lifted the pipe and puckered his lips

come and do a jig with us

he invited all the people

began cheering and clapping

Name: _____   **Date:** _____

Reread the story below, The Singing King. Circle all the words that have ing in it.

King Simon loved to sing. He liked to call himself a songbird. But no one in his kingdom liked his singing. And no one wanted to tell King Simon that his singing was awful.

"Please do something, Queen Dora!" the people begged, holding both ears. "The king squawks like a chicken when he sings!"

"I have tried and tried to get him to stop," said the queen. "But he just loves to sing. Perhaps someone else will have better luck."

Some people came up with ideas. A lad said, "King Simon, it is more fun to make bubbles than to sing. I have some soap and a bubble pipe for you. Watch me. Here is all you need to do."

The king lifted the pipe and puckered his lips. He and the lad sent hundreds of bubbles into the air.

King Simon watched the bubbles float in the sunshine. The bubbles were so big and pink, they made the king feel like singing. But his song was so awful that it made all the bubbles go pop, pop, pop!

A swimmer told the king to take up swimming. "It will be much more fun than singing," he said.

King Simon agreed and went to a lake. But as soon as the king jumped in the warm water, he felt like singing.

"Tra-la-la, tra-la-la, GLUB-GLUB-Glub!" the king sang. His song was so awful that all the fish began to leap out of the lake. PLOP! PLOP! SPLOT! One by one the fish landed on the shore.

Three children called the king to come out of the water. "King Simon, come and do a jig with us," the children said. "A jig is more fun than singing or swimming."

Name: _____   **Date:** _____

"A fine idea!" the king said with a grin. He called out his band. He invited all the people of the town to come.

King Simon began hopping up and down. But then he started to sing, too! His singing was so awful that all the people began running home! Do you think King Simon stopped singing?

Yes, he did. He sat down all alone on a bench. After a while, a little girl came along. Tugging on his sleeve, she said, "King Simon, just hum. Humming is more fun, and it's almost like singing."

King Simon nodded at the little girl and started humming. They began to hum together. His humming was perfect!

The people came back and began cheering and clapping. They began humming, too!

Before long, the king and all the people were humming all day. People came from far and near to the kingdom to hear the humming. But best of all, King Simon never sang again.

How many words with ing did you find? _____

Answer the following questions in complete sentences.

1. Who tried to get the king to stop singing? _____

_____

2. Why did the people like his humming? _____

_____

Name: _____   **Date:** _____

Story Mapping

Story Title: _____

Setting – (where and when)

_____

_____

_____

_____

Characters – (who)

_____

_____

_____

_____

Problem – (what problem did the character/s have)

_____

_____

_____

_____

Solution – (how the problem was solved)

_____

_____

_____

_____

Ending – (can be the lesson of the story)

_____

_____

_____

_____

Spelling

Name: _____　　　　**Date:** _____

Spelling List

Adding ing

1. match
2. matching
3. help
4. helping
5. munch
6. munching
7. bend
8. bending
9. fast
10. fasting

Extra Credit

1. October
2. Sunday
3. singing

Fill in the blanks using the words from the spelling list.

- It is not very nice to _____ on a bag of chips in front of someone who is _____. That loud _____ sound will probably make him look at his watch to check when the _____ will be over.

- There are many ways to _____ your mother. One way may be to simply _____ down and pick up something that may have dropped. _____ down can be really easy for a kid but quite hard for someone older.

- Another form of _____ around the house can be with laundry. You can _____ the freshly laundered socks by looking to see which ones have the same pattern. Then be sure to check if they are the same size. _____ socks can be tricky at times if there are a few sizes with the same pattern.

- In the month of _____ the girls high school puts on a play with a lot of _____. They spend every _____ practicing.

Name: _____   **Date:** _____

Spelling Review Sheet

Word Box

match matching help helping munch munching bend bending
fast fasting October Sunday singing

I. Sort the Spelling Words:

Words with one syllable	Words with two syllables
_____	_____
_____	_____
_____	_____
_____	_____
_____	_____
	_____
	_____

Circle the /ing/ in each word. **Underline** the root words.

Name: _____   **Date:** _____

Spelling Workheet

> Word Box
>
> match   matching   help   helping   munch   munching   bend   bending
>
> fast   fasting   October   Sunday   singing

II. Correct the misspelled words:

mach _____   mnching _____   fasting _____

maching _____   bend _____   sondae _____

hlep _____   bnding _____   seengeeng _____

hlping _____   fest _____   mnch _____

actowber _____

III. Find the synonym (word with a similar meaning)

1. chewing   _____

2. assisting   _____

3. twisting   _____

4. similar   _____

5. speedy   _____

Name: _____   **Date:** _____

Spelling Workheet

Word Box

match matching help helping munch munching bend bending
fast fasting October Sunday singing

IV. Complete the analogies using words from the spelling list.

1. Bend is to _____ ,as stand is to standing.

2. Open is to close, as _____ to slow.

3. Gum is to chew, as cracker is to _____.

4. Feet is to dancing, as voice is to _____.

5. Light bulb is to light, as _____ is to fire.

V. Connect the syllables to make words. Then write the words on the lines.

bend	ing	1. _____
munch	ing	2. _____
match	ing	3. _____
Sun	ing	4. _____
sing	day	5. _____

Word Work

B
A
C

Name: _____   **Date:** _____

Word Work

Syllabication: Chunk each word into smaller parts. (Hint; spot the vowels first). Each part should have a vowel and a consonant after it.

words	syllable 1	syllable 2	syllable 3
himself	him	self	
singbird			
awful			
something			
chicken			
perhaps			
someone			
better			
bubble			
sunshine			

Some words above are compound words (a word made up of two small words. Can you find the compound words? Circle them if you can.

Name: _____   **Date:** _____

Word Work

Suffixes and Root Words: Chunk each word into root words and suffixes.

words	root word	suffix
singing	sing	ing
holding		
swimming		
hopping		
running		
tugging		
humming		
cheering		
clapping		
stopping		

Which words have a double consonant before the suffix?

_____

Do you know the rule? Yes or no

Name: _____

Date: _____

Add the doing suffix to the following root words. Don't forget to double the consonant when necessary.

1. snack= _snacking_ _____

2. drink= _____

3. slip= _____

4. trick= _____

5. track= _____

6. fish= _____

7. map= _____

8. drop= _____

9. spill= _____

10. win= _____

Create your own list of 1-1-1 words:

1. _____

2. _____

3. _____

4. _____

5. _____

Name: _____   **Date:** _____

Add the suffix ing to each word. Make changes when necessary. Then sort the root words in the chart below.

beg*ging*	bang	dig	rip	snap	snip
hand	start	spend	spot	run	last
list	sit	send	brush	catch	tap
rant	rent	risk	grab	grin	trash

Root words with no change	Root Words with 1-1-1 rule
bang	beg
_____	_____
_____	_____
_____	_____
_____	_____
_____	_____
_____	_____
_____	_____
_____	_____
_____	_____

Name: _____　　**Date:** _____

Word Work

Suffixes and Root Words: Chunk each word into root words and suffixes.

words	root word	suffix
hoping	hope	ing
driving		
making		
smiling		
moving		
coming		
having		
living		
giving		
baking		

Do you know the rule? Yes or no

_____

Name: _____ **Date:** _____

Add the doing suffix to the following root words. Don't forget to drop the silent e when necessary.

1. hope= _hoping_____

2. smoke=_____

3. hint= _____

4. hide= _____

5. pinch= _____

6. pile= _____

7. smile= _____

8. file= _____

9. fill= _____

10. wine= _____

Create your own list of words that end with silent e:

1. _____

2. _____

3. _____

4. _____

Name: _____   **Date:** _____

Add the suffix **ing** to each word. Make changes when necessary. Then sort the root words in the chart below.

bike̸ing	like	lick	swipe	whip	snip
hand	start	fly	ride	drive	dive
swim	kite	rake	brush	catch	tap
tap	fake	fast	grab	grind	rise

Root words with no change	Root Words with 1-1-1 rule	Root Words ending with e
lick	whip	bike
_____	_____	_____
_____	_____	_____
_____	_____	_____
_____	_____	_____
_____		_____
		_____
		_____

Name: _____   **Date:** _____

Street of Flowers

Completion of work: _____

Neatness: _____

Mastery of skills: _____

Pages _____ – not done in class.

Pages _____ – homework (in HW booklet)

Grade: 3
Volume: 11

Parents signature: _____

Reading

Name: _____ **Date:** _____

Street of Flowers

handed her husband a spade

my husband hammered and sawed

on the porch railing

sprinkled the little plants with water

some lumber left in the basement

Zelda's mother and father were pleased

Name: _____   Date: _____

Reread the story below, Street of Flowers. Underline any phrase you recognize from preparation for reading. Circle all the words that have a suffix -ing or -ed at the end.

One spring morning, Zelda was sitting on her front porch. She saw Mr. and Mrs. Kaminski across the street. Mrs. Kaminski handed her husband a spade. Zelda wondered what they were going to do.

"Hi," yelled Zelda.

"Come on over," called Mrs. Kaminski. "Come and see what we are doing."

Zelda smiled and walked across the street.

"The porch and front yard have needed cheering up for a long time," said Mrs. Kaminski. "These flowers on the porch will do the trick."

"Last week my husband hammered and sawed and made this flower box for me," she said. "I'm going to fill it with flowers and put it on the porch railing. Do you want to help me?"

"Yes!" said Zelda.

They worked hard filling the flower box with dirt. Next Zelda dug small holes in the dirt. Mrs. Kaminski planted a flower in each hole. Zelda sprinkled the little plants with water.

"I wish we had flowers like these," said Zelda.

"You can make a flower box," said Mr. Kaminski. "I still have some lumber left in the basement."

He showed Zelda what to do with the lumber. She smiled and thanked him when the flower box was finished.

Mrs. Kaminski gave Zelda some of her purple flowers. Zelda planted them in her box and watered them. Zelda's mother and father were pleased when Zelda came home with her flower box.

Name: _____ **Date:** _____

"I'm glad you made it," said her mother.

"Your flowers add a lot to this porch," her father said. "I wish the rest of the street had flowers, too."

"What if we invite people on the block to come over?" asked Zelda. "We can show them the flowers."

Mother, Father, and Zelda walked to one home after the other.

"Please come to see the flowers," they said to the people.

The people came. The next week, they began making flower boxes, too. They dug and planted. They smiled and joked. They helped one another.

The flowers cheered up the block and the people, too. Zelda's street was like one long flower garden.

How many words with the ing suffix did you find? _____

How many words with the ed suffix did you find? _____

Answer the following questions in complete sentences.

1. Why did Mrs. Kaminski want to plant flowers? _____

_____

2. Why did the people plant flowers on the block?_____

_____

Name: _____ **Date:** _____

Story Mapping

Story Title: _____

Setting – (where and when)

_____
_____
_____
_____
_____

Characters – (who)

_____
_____
_____
_____
_____

Problem – (what problem did the character/s have)

_____
_____
_____
_____
_____

Solution – (how the problem was solved)

_____
_____
_____
_____
_____

Ending – (can be the lesson of the story)

_____
_____
_____
_____
_____

Spelling

B
A
C

Name: _____   Date: _____

Spelling List

<u>Adding ing</u>

1. win
2. winning
3. shop
4. shopping
5. drag
6. dragging
7. sled
8. sledding
9. swim
10. swimming

<u>Extra Credit</u>

1. November
2. Monday
3. morning

Use 10 spelling words to fill in the blanks.

- In the winter children can have a really fun time. If there is snow on the ground they can use a _____ to go _____. They can _____ their sleds to the top of a hill or any place that has a slope for this fun activity. _____ the sled can be hard work, but the fun of coming down makes it well worth the effort.

- In the summer children can have a really fun time going _____ in an outdoor pool. When it is really hot outside there is no better way to cool off. Some people enjoy going for a _____ even in the winter, in an indoor heated pool.

- The spring and fall weather would probably _____ everyone's vote as favorite weather. Getting out of bed on a beautiful spring _____ is probably easier than in the cold winter, or hot summer.

- When one goes to a _____ he can say that he is going _____.

Name: _____   **Date:** _____

Spelling Review Sheet

> Word Box
>
> win   winning   shop   shopping   drag   dragging   sled   sledding   swim
> swimming   November   Monday   morning

I. Sort the Spelling Words:

Words with one syllable	Words with two syllables	Words with three syllables
_____	_____	_____
_____	_____	
_____	_____	
_____	_____	
_____	_____	
	_____	
	_____	

Circle the /ng/ in each word.

Underline the words that have /ng/ as part of a suffix. **Box** the suffix in those words. **Write** the root words here; _____ ,

_____ , _____ , _____ ,

_____

How many syllables do these root words have? _____

How many vowels do these root words have? _____

How many consonants are there after the vowel in these root words? _____

Name: _____

Date: _____

Spelling Worksheet

Word Box

win   winning   shop   shopping   drag   dragging   sled   sledding   swim
swimming   November   Monday   morning

II. Correct the misspelled words.

win _____   shopp _____   shoping _____

wining _____   jrag _____   jraging _____

seld _____   selding _____   swm _____

swming _____   nvmbr _____   mundai _____

moorning _____

III. Find the synonym (word with a similar meaning):

1. victory   _____

2. haul   _____

3. sleigh   _____

4. store   _____

5. sunrise   _____

Name: _____   **Date:** _____

Spelling Workheet

> **Word Box**
>
> win winning shop shopping drag dragging sled sledding swim
> swimming November Monday morning

IV. Complete the analogies using words from the spelling list.

1. Happy is to sad, as _____ win _____ is to lose.

2. _____ is to water, as _____ is to snow.

3. Shoving is to pushing, as _____ is to pulling.

4. _____ is to first, as _____ is to second.

5. Camping is to campground, as _____ is to store.

6. April is to spring, as _____ is to fall.

V. Connect the syllables to make words. Then write the words on the lines.

win	ging	1. _____
shop	ding	2. _____
drag	ming	3. _____
sled	ping	4. _____
swim	ning	5. _____

Word Work

B
A
C

Name: _____   Date: _____

Word Work

Syllabication: Chunk each word into smaller parts. (Hint; spot the vowels first). Some syllables may have two vowels in it (such as; rail, vite)

words	syllable 1	syllable 2	syllable 3
morning	morn	ing	
across			
husband			
flowers			
railing			
lumber			
purple			
invite			
wagon			

Which type of vowel do the syllables with two vowels have?

short or long

Name: _____   **Date:** _____

Add the past tense suffix to the following root words. Don't forget to double the consonant when necessary.

1. work= ___worked_____

2. finish= _____

3. watch= _____

4. cross= _____

5. cheer=_____

6. clean= _____

7. rain= _____

8. stop= _____

9. wag= _____

10. plan=_____

Create your own list of 1-1-1 words:

1. _____

2. _____

3. _____

4. _____

Name: _____   **Date:** _____

Add the suffix **ed** to each word. Make changes when necessary. Then sort the root words in the chart below.

beg*ged*	bang	dig	rip	snap	snip
hand	start	spend	spot	run	last
list	sit	send	brush	catch	tap
rant	rent	risk	grab	grin	trash

Root words with no change	Root Words with 1-1-1 rule
bang	*beg*

Name: _____   **Date:** _____

Can You Tell?
–
Bird Feet

Completion of work: _____

Neatness: _____

Mastery of skills: _____

Pages _____ – not done in class.

Pages _____ – homework (in HW booklet)

Grade: 3
Volume: 12

Parents signature: _____

Reading

Name: _____   Date: _____

Reread the poem below. (1) Circle all the words that have the suffix er. (2) Underline all the words that have an r controlled vowel. (3) Then answer the questions that the poem asks.

Can You Tell?

When do the robins first chirp and sing,

Winter, Summer, fall, or spring?   _____

When is it hotter than spring or fall,

And the sun shines longer and the grass gets tall? _____

When do the oak leaves show deep red,

And blossoms die in the flower bed?   _____

When can skaters glide fast on the lakes,

And children slide in the soft snowflakes?   _____

Name: _____   **Date:** _____

Reread the article below. (1) Circle all the words that have an added suffix of -ing. (2) Underline all the words that have an r controlled vowel.

Bird Feet

All birds have two feet. Most birds have the same number of toes (4). All birds have a claw at the tip of each toe.

A perching bird has a toe at the back for hanging on.

Some birds have two toes in front and two in back for going up tree trunks.

Scratching birds have toes like a rake.

Swimming birds have feet like paddles.

Birds that eat fish and meat have big toes and claws for grabbing.

These are drawings of five different kinds of bird feet. Which ones have you seen?

Vocabulary Development

Draw a picture of a toe with a **claw** at the end.	Draw a picture of a **paddle**.

Word Work

Name: _____ **Date:** _____

Word Work

Suffixes and Root Words: Chunk each word into suffixes and root words.

words	root word	suffix
pleased	please	ed
waved		
smiled		
joked		
shared		
baked		
piled		
liked		
ruled		
sneezed		

Do you know the rule? Yes or no

_____

Name: _____   **Date:** _____

Add the doing suffix to the following root words. Don't forget to drop the silent e when necessary.

1. hope= ___hoping___

2. smoke=_____

3. hint= _____

4. hide= _____

5. pinch= _____

6. pile= _____

7. smile= _____

8. file= _____

9. fill= _____

10. wine= _____

Create your own list of words that end with silent e:

1. _____

2. _____

3. _____

4. _____

Name: _____   **Date:** _____

Word Work

Suffixes and Root Words: Chunk each word into suffixes and root words.

words	root word	suffix
sitting	sit	ing
going		
cheering		
smiled		
joked		
walked		
planted		
cheered		
pleased		
watered		

Which word has a double consonant before the suffix? _____

Which words had a silent e that was dropped? _____

_____ , _____ .

Name: _____ **Date:** _____

Add the suffix **ed** to each word. Make changes when necessary. Then sort the root words in the chart below.

bike͏ed	like	lick	swipe	whip	snip
hand	start	plant	wipe	mail	smoke
tape	check	rake	brush	sneeze	tap
tap	fake	feast	grab	pave	cool

Root words with no change	Root Words with 1-1-1 rule	Root Words ending with e
lick	whip	bike

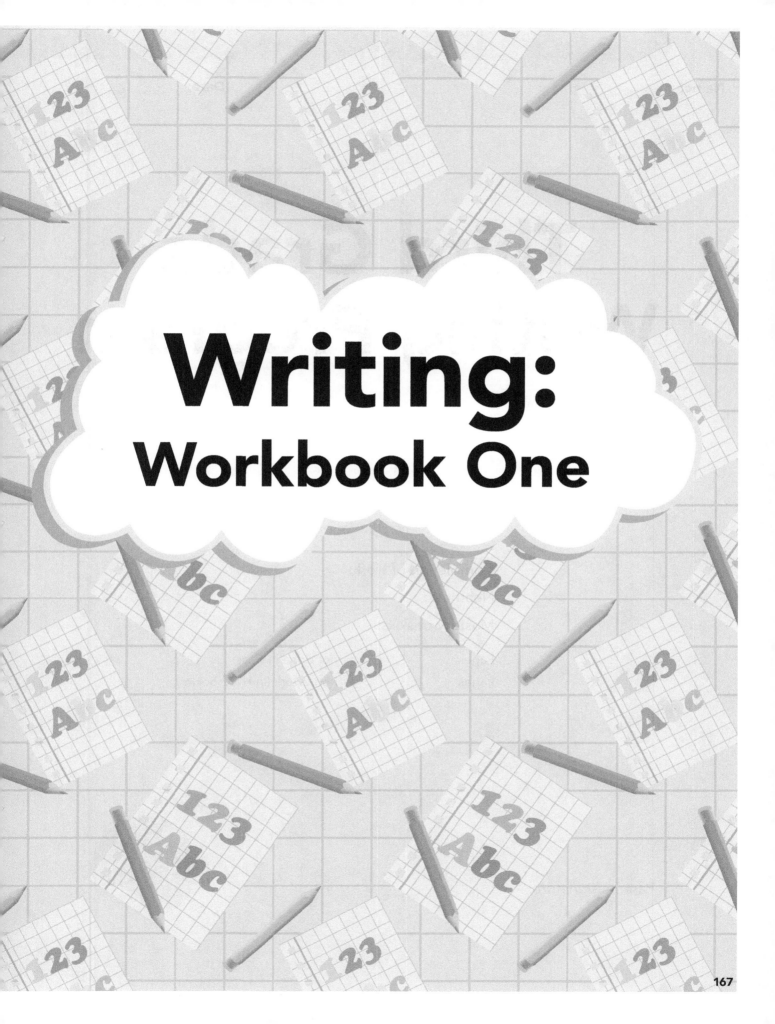

Writing:
Workbook One

Name: _____   **Date:** _____

Third Grade Writing Program

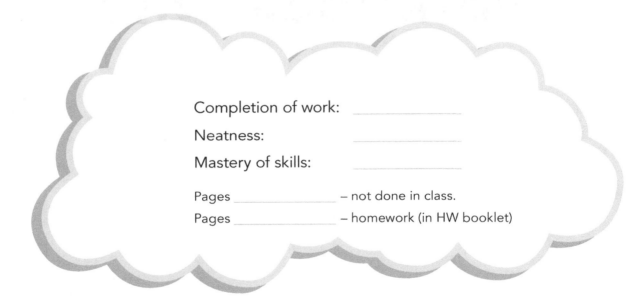

Completion of work: _____

Neatness: _____

Mastery of skills: _____

Pages _____ – not done in class.

Pages _____ – homework (in HW booklet)

Part 1

Parents signature: _____

Name: _____　　　　　**Date:** _____

Sentence Work

A sentence is a group of words that tells or asks something. It stands for a complete thought.

EXAMPLES; Friends play. Cars go fast.

Make a check if the group of words is a sentence. Make an x of the group of words is not a sentence.

1. _____X_____ A long time ago.

2. _____ The class went to the park.

3. _____ Near the tree.

4. _____ Ten children played.

5. _____ Mark hit the ball.

6. _____ A dog chased the ball.

7. _____ Bill and Tom.

8. _____ Ran and played all day.

9. _____ Everyone had fun.

10. _____ Jan lost a new red shoe.

11. _____ We ate lunch.

12. _____ Too hot for us.

13. _____ The boys and girls talked.

14. _____ Some people.

15. _____ Sang songs.

16. _____ Then we went home.

Name: _____　　　Date: _____

The **characters** are the _____ who a story is about. The **main character** tells us who a story is mostly about. Sometimes animals are considered characters in a story as well.

"I am hungry," said a lion. "I'll go and get a rabbit to eat." The lion got a rabbit. The lion looked up. "Here comes a big deer," he said. "I'll go and get the deer. This rabbit is too little." And he let the rabbit go. Away went the deer. Away went the rabbit. Away went the lion. The deer ran and ran, and the lion ran after it. The deer ran fast…and it got away! The lion came back to get the rabbit. "My rabbit has gone! It has gone!" said the lion. And he had to stay hungry.

Who are the **characters** in the story above? _____ ,

_____ , _____

Who is the **main character** in the story above?

_____

The **setting** tells us when and where. Some examples of **when** are; time of _____ , month or season of the _____ , a period in history (ie; early nineteen hundreds, before WWII), an amount of time etc. Some examples of **where** are; name of _____ or any other place, room in the _____ , outside or inside, type of place (ie; dessert, forest, city) etc.

Name: _____   **Date:** _____

When; Use a when word or phrase to answer the following questions.

1. **When** is your birthday? _____

2. **When** is your next dentist appointment? _____

3. **When** is Pesach? _____

4. **When** was the airplane invented? _____

5. **When** did the United States become a country? _____

6. **When** is the next presidential election? _____

7. **When** is recess? _____

Where; Use a where word or phrase to answer the following questions.

1. **Where** do you live? _____

2. **Where** is your school located? _____

3. **Where** do you keep your family pictures? _____

4. **Where** do your grandparents live? _____

5. **Where** did you go on Chol Hamoed? _____

6. **Where** in the world is the tallest building? _____

7. **Where** do lions and tigers mostly live? _____

Name: _____   **Date:** _____

The word **what** tells us what happened in the story. It tells us **what** the story is about, including the main idea and supporting details. Read the following passage, then answer the questions that follow.

Bees live in a house that is called a hive. There are three kinds of bees: workers, drones, and queens. Only one queen bee can live in each hive. If she is lost or dead, the other bees will stop their work.

Bees are very wise and busy little creatures. They all join together to build cells of wax for their honey. Each bee takes its proper place, and does its own work. Some go out and gather honey from the flowers; others stay at home and work inside the hive.

The cells which they build, are all of one shape and size, and no room is left between them. The cells are not round, but have six sides.

Did you ever look into a glass hive to see the bees while at work? It is pleasant to see how busy they always are.

But the drones do not work. Before winter comes, all the drones are driven from the hive so that they may not eat the honey which they did not gather.

It is not quite safe for children to handle bees. They have sharp stings that they use in their defense.

What is the story about? _____

_____

What do they do all day? _____

_____

What happens to the drones before the winter comes? _____

_____

What is the warning at the end of the passage for children? _____

_____

Name: _____   **Date:** _____

Movement is a word that is used to describe action. It tells us what someone did, is doing, or will do.

Robbie was born in a cozy den high in Father Oak's sturdy trunk. In the spring, he learned to climb on Father Oak's strong branches. All summer long he played with his friends Chip and Blackbird in the shade of Father Oak's green leaves.

On the first day of fall, Robbie woke early, kissed his mother, and tiptoed out to find Chip.

What are some of the **movements** that Robbie did in the passage above?

_____

_____

Sound is a word used to describe anything which can be heard.

Robbie Raccoon loved his home. He loved the long swishy grass, the sparkling stream, and the rustling trees. But most of all, Robbie loved Old Father Oak…

"Robbie, what are you doing?" asked his friend Chip…

What are some of the **sounds** that can be heard in the passage above?

_____

Name: _____   Date: _____

A Picture can tell A Thousand Words

1. Here is a title for this picture _____ Back to School _____

2. Here are some details about the topic <u>Back to School</u>. Use the picture to help you think of more ideas;
    *   I am sitting on a bus
    *   after the summer
    *   children are all excited
    *   children talk to their friends about their summer
    *   children cannot stay in their seats
    *   everyone is going up a grade
    *   early in September
    *   children are laughing
    *   children have new shoes
    *   children have new school supplies
    *   children are full of hope for the new year
    *   _____
    *   _____

3. Sort the details above, in the preparation for writing chart, on the next page.

Name: _____   **Date:** _____

Preparation for Writing;

Characters and Setting (who, when, and where)	What
_____	_____
_____	_____
_____	_____
_____	_____
_____	_____

Title
_____

Movement/sound	Feeling/Mood
_____	_____
_____	_____
_____	_____
_____	_____

> Read the paragraph below.   The sentences are labeled;   **1 – title/topic sentence,**
> **2 – characters and setting sentence, 3 – sentence that tells what, 4 – movement**
> **sound sentence, 5 – feeling/ wrap up sentence**

[1] I am on the school bus with many other children in my neighborhood. [2] It is early in September and we are going back to school. [3] We have new briefcases with our new supplies. [4] We cannot sit still. [4] We talk to our friends all about the fun summer we had. [5] We are all full of hope that we will have a good year.

Name: _____   Date: _____

Sentence Work

- **Begin** a sentence with a capital letter, and **end** a sentence with a period. EXAMPLE: **N**ow Deb and Jet play together.

Rewrite these sentences. Use proper beginning and ending punctuation.

1. deb likes to play ball

_____

2. her ball is red

_____

3. jet wants to play

_____

4. deb throws the ball

_____

5. jet likes the ball

_____

6. the ball goes far

_____

7. jet runs to the ball

_____

8. jet brings the ball back

_____

Name: _____   **Date:** _____

9.   deb hugs her dog

_____

10. they have fun together

_____

11. patty played on the baseball team

_____

12. she played hard

_____

13. she hit two home runs

_____

- Put a question mark (?) at the end of a sentence that asks something.
  EXAMPLE: Is he your brother**?**

Rewrite these asking sentences using proper beginning and ending punctuation.

1.   what time is it

_____

2.   is it time for lunch

_____

3.   are you ready to eat

_____

4.   do you like apples

Name: _____   **Date:** _____

A Picture can tell A Thousand Words

1. Here is a title for this picture _____ *Fun at School* _____

2. Here are some details about the topic <u>Fun at School</u>. Use the picture to help you think of more ideas;

    - recess time
    - playing ball
    - schmoozing with friends
    - school yard
    - some boys are lonely
    - some boys are playing together
    - the boys are playing hard
    - team effort
    - _____
    - _____

3. Sort the details above, in the preparation for writing chart, on the next page.

Name: _____   **Date:** _____

Preparation for Writing;

Characters and Setting (who, when, and where)	What
_____	_____
_____	_____
_____	_____
_____	_____

Title
_____

Movement/sound	Feeling/Mood
_____	_____
_____	_____
_____	_____
_____	_____

Read the paragraph below. Label the sentences;   1 – **title/topic sentence,**
2 – **characters and setting sentence,** 3 – **sentence that tells what,** 4 – **movement
sound sentence,** 5 – **feeling/ wrap up sentence**

At recess time, the boys in my class play in the school yard. Some boys play a fun game of ball. Other kids like to schmooze with their friends. The ball players play really hard for their team. The schmoozers are laughing and making funny faces. Most boys are having lots of fun during recess.

Name: _____   **Date:** _____

Sentence Work

Words in a sentence must be in an order that makes sense.
EXAMPLES: Grandpa plays baseball.
             My sister writes stories.

- **Write these words in an order that makes sense.**

1. brother My apples eats

    My brother eats apples.

2. drinks Elizabeth milk

    _____

3. butter peanut Kim likes

    _____

4. Justin bread wants

    _____

5. corn plants Chris

    _____

6. a fish Chang caught

    _____

7. breakfast cooks Dad

    _____

8. his shares Shawn lunch

    _____

9. the Rosa grew carrot

    _____

Name: _____   Date: _____

Sentence Work

A sentence is a group of words that tells or asks something. It stands for a complete thought.

EXAMPLES; Friends play. Cars go fast.

Draw lines between the groups of words to make sentences. Then read the sentences.

Our school	was climbing a tree.
Jennifer	went on a picnic.
The sun	shone all day.
Mrs. Brown	live in our building.
Our building	is made of wood.
Four families	lives on my street.
Corn and beans	fed the baby goat.
The wagon	has a broken wheel.
The mother goat	grow on a farm.
The boat	sailed in strong winds.
The fisher	were sold in the store.
Some of the fish	caught seven fish.
Our team	hit the ball a lot.
Our batters	won ten games.
The ballpark	was full of fans.

Name: _____   **Date:** _____

A Picture can tell A Thousand Words

1. Here is a title for this picture _____ Hard at Work _____

2. Here are some details about the topic <u>Hard at Work</u>. Use the picture to help you think of more ideas;
   - learning with peers
   - writing
   - thinking
   - listening
   - talking it over
   - asking questions
   - low whispering
   - team effort
   - _____
   - _____

3. Sort the details above, in the preparation for writing chart, on the next page.

Name: _____　　　　**Date:** _____

Preparation for Writing;

Characters and Setting (who, when, and where)	What
_____	_____
_____	_____
_____	_____
_____	_____

Title
_____

Movement/sound	Feeling/Mood
_____	_____
_____	_____
_____	_____
_____	_____

Read the paragraph below. Label the sentences; **1 – title/topic sentence, 2 – characters and setting sentence, 3 – sentence that tells what, 4 – movement sound sentence, 5 – feeling/ wrap up sentence**

At school my teacher has us learn in groups of two. We share the learning with our partner. One boy is talking while the other is listening. One boy is asking questions and the other boy tries to answer. One boy is writing and the other boy is reading. There is a hum of low murmuring heard in the classroom. We are all hard at work.

Name: _____   Date: _____

Sentence Work

- Write <u>S</u> if the group of words is a sentence. Write <u>N</u> if the group of words is not a sentence.

    1. _____ A lizard is.

    2. _____ Reptiles are cold-blooded.

    3. _____ Snakes do not have eyelids.

    4. _____ Found in warm places.

- Draw lines between the groups of words to make sentences.

1. Alan and Ellen	teaches them how to play.
2. The big game	is Sunday night.
3. Their coach	play on the same team.
4. The phone	is calling from Toronto.
5. Our uncle	rush to answer it.
6. Betty and Tom	rings.
7. The hungry frog	ate an insect.
8. Twenty geese	is fun to watch.
9. A beetle	flew south for the winter.

- Write the words in an order that makes sense. Don't forget punctuation.

    1. I best friend have a

    _____

    2. together our bikes We ride

    _____

    3. We climb sometimes trees

    _____

Name: _____   **Date:** _____

Sentence Work

Write sentences. Write a telling sentence describing an object. A telling sentence begins with a _____ and ends with a

_____ .

- Write a sentence about your birthday. My birthday is in the month of January.

  _____

  _____

- Write a sentence about where you live. I live in an apartment building with five floors.

  _____

  _____

- Write a sentence about your family. My family has mostly boys.

  _____

  _____

Name: _____   **Date:** _____

A Picture can tell A Thousand Words

1. Here is a title for this picture _____ My Day Off _____

2. Here are some details about the topic <u>My Day Off</u>. Use the picture to help you think of more ideas;

   - sick at home
   - holiday vacation
   - bored
   - eating
   - reading
   - _____
   - _____
   - _____
   - _____

3. Sort the details above, in the preparation for writing chart, on the next page.

Name: _____   **Date:** _____

Preparation for Writing;

Characters and Setting (who, when, and where)	What
_____	_____
_____	_____
_____	_____
_____	_____

Title
_____

Movement/sound	Feeling/Mood
_____	_____
_____	_____
_____	_____
_____	_____

Name: _____   **Date:** _____

Complete the paragraph using the chart above. Use the checklist to check your writing when you are done.

Read the paragraph below. Label the sentences; **1 – title/topic sentence, 2 – characters and setting sentence, 3 – sentence that tells what, 4 – movement sound sentence, 5 – feeling/ wrap up sentence**

- You can have more than one sentence with a number 3 or 4 label, as they are details about the main idea.

One day I was home from school with a low fever. I woke up late and ate a warm breakfast. _____

_____

_____

_____

_____

_____

_____

_____

Writing checklist;

☐ My paragraph begins with a main idea sentence.

☐ All my sentences begin with a capital and end with a period.

☐ My paragraph includes three details telling about the main idea.

☐ My paragraph ends with a wrap up feeling sentence.

☐ I checked my spelling.

Name: _____   **Date:** _____

Sentence Work

A **telling sentence** is a group of words that tells something.

EXAMPLES; I fed my pony.

Ponies like to run and play.

- **Write telling on the line before the group of words if it is a telling sentence. Leave the line blank if it is not a sentence.**

_____telling_____   1. A long time ago.

_____   2. Josh loves his pony.

_____   3. His name is Zip.

_____   4. Fast horses.

_____   5. Zip can run fast.

_____   6. He eats apples.

_____   7. Over the hill.

_____   8. Zip runs to Josh.

_____   9. Zip has a long tail.

_____   10. Josh and his mother.

_____   11. His hair is soft.

_____   12. After school.

_____   13. Josh likes to play with Zip.

_____   14. In the barn.

_____   15. Josh brushes Zip.

_____   16. You can ride Zip, too.

Name: _____　　　**Date:** _____

Sentence Work

Write sentences. Write a telling sentence describing an object.
A telling sentence begins with a _____ and ends with
a _____ .

- Write a sentence about your favorite food. My most favorite food is pancakes.

  | **ice cream** | **milk chocolate** | **marble cake** | **cookies** |

  _____

  _____

- Write a sentence about your favorite game. Monopoly is my best game to play
  with my friends.

  | **uno** | **checkers** | **sorry** | **connect four** | **chutes and ladders** |

  _____

  _____

- Write a sentence about your favorite sport.   I am the best soccer player in
  my class.

  | **baseball** | **basketball** | **football** | **jump rope** |

  _____

  _____

Name: _____   **Date:** _____

Sentence Work

An asking sentence is a group of words if it is an asking sentence. Leave the line blank if the group of words is not a sentence.

EXAMPLES; How old are you? Where do you live?

- **Write <u>asking</u> on the line before the group of words if it is an asking sentence. Leave the line blank if the group of words is not a sentence.**

_____asking_____	1. Is this your friend?
_____	2. Where does she live?
_____	3. She is in town?
_____	4. How was school today?
_____	5. Music and art?
_____	6. Do you want a snack?
_____	7. Where are the apples?
_____	8. Look in the?
_____	9. When does school begin?
_____	10. Do you have any brothers?
_____	11. Where can we work?
_____	12. The kitchen in?
_____	13. Can you ride a bike?
_____	14. Yes, I?
_____	15. Why did Sarah cry?

Name: _____   Date: _____

Sentence Work

Write sentences. Remember that a sentence tells a complete thought. A asking sentence begins with a _____ and ends with an _____ .

- A new boy joined your class. Write a sentence asking him something about himself. Where did you go to school last year?

Where....	When....	Who.....	what....	Why...

_____

_____

- Your friend came over to your house. Write a question you would ask him. What game would you like to play?

game	food	go	time	drink	sport

_____

_____

- Your grandfather came to your house for shabbos. Write a question you would ask him. Who was your rebbe when you were my age?

learn	shul	help	play	sleep

_____

_____

Name: _____   **Date:** _____

A Picture can tell A Thousand Words

1. Here is a title for this picture _____ School Lunch

2. Here are some details about the topic <u>School Lunch</u>. Use the picture to help you think of more ideas;

    -   we eat in the lunchroom
    -   sitting with friends
    -   tasty and healthy food
    -   crunching and munching
    -   French fries and pizza
    -   _____
    -   _____
    -   _____
    -   _____

3. Sort the details above, in the preparation for writing chart, on the next page.

Name: _____   **Date:** _____

Preparation for Writing;

Characters and Setting (who, when, and where)	What
_____	_____
_____	_____
_____	_____
_____	_____

Title
_____

Movement/sound	Feeling/Mood
_____	_____
_____	_____
_____	_____
_____	_____

Name: _____   **Date:** _____

Complete the paragraph using the chart above. Use the checklist to check your writing when you are done.

> Read the paragraph below. Label the sentences;   **1 – title/topic sentence,**
> **2 – characters and setting sentence, 3 – sentence that tells what, 4 – movement sound sentence, 5 – feeling/ wrap up sentence**

- Sometimes sentence number one can actually be labeled 2, and sentence number 2 can be labeled 1.

- You can have more than one sentence with a number 3 or 4 label, as they are details about the main idea.

After working hard all morning I get to eat a healthy and tasty lunch at school. _____

_____

_____

_____

_____

_____

_____

Writing checklist;

☐ My paragraph begins with a main idea sentence.

☐ All my sentences begin with a capital and end with a period.

☐ My paragraph includes three details telling about the main idea.

☐ My paragraph ends with a wrap up feeling sentence.

☐ I checked my spelling.

Name: _____   **Date:** _____

Sentence Work

- **Write <u>asking</u> on the line before the group of words if it is an asking sentence. Leave the line blank if the group of words is not a sentence.**

_____asking_____   1. Where is the toy store?

_____   2. The toy store is near school.

_____   3. Do you like kites?

_____   4. There are balloons and balls.

_____   5. Some toys can play music.

_____   6. Who plays with markers?

_____   7. I have a few games.

_____   8. Mom will buy a puzzle.

_____   9. Where are the bikes?

_____   10. When will you play with bubbles?

- **Read the sentences. Write each sentence under the correct heading.**

I went to the toy store.   Are there any puzzles?

Which toy do you want?   I picked a game.

Telling sentences

1. _____

2. _____

Asking sentences

1. _____

2. _____

Name: _____   **Date:** _____

Sentence Work

Write sentences. Write a telling sentence describing an object.
Then write an asking sentence about it.

- A round and colorful object which is used for playing. What can it be?
  <u>A ball</u>

> **Something that is used for playing**

_____

_____

- A black and white animal with four legs which can be found in Africa.
  Which animal fits that description? <u>a zebra</u>

> **an animal**

_____

_____

- An ice cold food which is hard and tastes really sweet. What can it be?
  <u>ices</u>

> **a food**

_____

_____

Made in the USA
Middletown, DE
13 September 2024